About Albert Camus: The Man Behind the Myth

Collection: What Do You Know?

Hichem Karoui

Global East-West for Research & Studies

Collection: What Do You Know?

ISBN (Print): 978-1-78795-077-1

Global East-West (London)

Contents

Introduction 1

1. Overview of Albert Camus's influence in literature and existential philosophy 7
2. Brief biography and historical context of his life and work 11
3. Early Life and Formative Years 17
4. Camus's childhood in Algeria, family background, and early experiences 23
5. Education and early exposure to philosophical ideas 27
6. The influence of Algerian culture and politics on his worldview 31
7. Camus's Philosophical Journey 35

8. Transition from journalism to literary and philosophical writing 39

9. Exploration of Camus's early philosophical essays and articles 45

10. Examination of his role in the French Resistance and its influence on his work 49

11. Major Works and Themes 55

12. In-depth analysis of "The Stranger" and the theme of absurdity 59

13. Exploration of "The Plague" as a reflection on human nature and morality 63

14. Discussion of "The Myth of Sisyphus" and Camus's concept of absurdism 67

15. Examination of "The Fall" and themes of guilt and judgment 71

16. Camus's Philosophy and Worldview 75

17. Exploration of absurdism and the human condition 81

18. Camus's thoughts on existentialism, freedom, and rebellion 85

19. The concept of the absurd hero in Camus's philosophy 89

20. Camus's Views on Morality and Justice 93
21. Style and Influence:A Literary Giant and Existential Thought Leader 97
22. Analysis of Camus's narrative techniques and stylistic choices 101
23. Camus's influence on modern literature and existential thought 105
24. Comparison with contemporary philosophers and writers 109
25. Camus's Political Engagements and Controversies 115
26. Camus's stance on colonialism and the Algerian War 119
27. Engagement with political and social issues of his time 125
28. Critiques and controversies surrounding his political views 131
29. Legacy and Contemporary Relevance 135
30. The enduring impact of Camus's ideas and writings 139
31. Camus's relevance in the contemporary philosophical and cultural landscape 143

32. Reflections on Camus's influence in current philosophical debates 147
33. Conclusion 153
34. Summarising Camus's contributions to philosophy and literature 159
35. Reflecting on the complexities and nuances of his legacy 163
36. Appendix 167
Timeline of Albert Camus's life 173
Glossary of key terms and concepts in Camus's work 179
Post-Scriptum 185
Bibliography 193

Introduction

Albert Camus, an eminent writer of the 20th century, left an indelible mark on literature and existential philosophy. His thought-provoking works and profound philosophical ideas continue to captivate and challenge readers. In this book, we will delve into the life, works, and worldview of Albert Camus, exploring the fascinating journey of this renowned writer.

Born on November 7, 1913, in Mondovi, French Algeria, Camus grew up in a working-class family. His father, Lucien Camus, who had fought in World War I, died when Albert was just one year old, leaving him with few memories but an everlasting sense of loss. This early tragedy profoundly impacted Camus, fostering a sense of alienation and a lifelong search for meaning. Raised by his illiterate mother, Catherine, who worked as a cleaning woman, Camus experienced the hardships of poverty and the resilience of the human spirit during his formative years.

Despite financial difficulties, Camus excelled academically, displaying an insatiable thirst for knowledge. He was granted a scholarship to pursue his education, which opened doors to a wider world and new intellectual horizons. While studying at the University of Algiers, philosophy captivated him, laying the foundation for his intellectual development. Here, he encountered the works of influential thinkers like Friedrich Nietzsche and Jean-Paul Sartre. Their philosophies and his experiences growing up in colonial Algeria shaped Camus's worldview and would later profoundly influence his literary creations.

Camus's early career began in journalism, where he used his writing to engage with pressing social and political issues. As a journalist, he travelled throughout Europe, reporting on events such as the Spanish Civil War and the rise of fascism. These experiences deepened his understanding of human nature and the world's complexities, laying the groundwork for his later literary and philosophical explorations.

While Camus's journalistic work allowed him to address societal concerns, he truly found his voice in his transition to fiction and philosophical writing. His first novel, "The Stranger" (1942), showcased his unique writing style and introduced readers to themes he would continue to explore throughout his career. This existential work portrays Meursault, a detached and indifferent protagonist, navigating the absurdity and meaninglessness of human existence. Through Meursault, Camus challenges the conventions of morality and societal norms, inviting readers to question the nature of truth and the value of individual experience.

In 1947, Camus published another groundbreaking novel, "The Plague." This allegorical tale explores a small Algerian town struck by a deadly epidemic, unmasking the human condition and exposing the complex interplay between suffering, morality, and heroism. Set amid World War II, "The Plague" reflects Camus's observations of the atrocities committed during the war and the existential crisis they created. The novel delves into the human capacity for solidarity and individual heroism in the face of overwhelming adversity, posing questions about resilience, hope, and the collective responsibility to confront societal challenges.

Camus's philosophical essays, including "The Myth of Sisyphus" (1942) and "The Rebel" (1951), further elucidated his philosophical ideas. In "The Myth of Sisyphus," Camus examines the absurdity of human existence and the necessity of embracing life's absurdities. He proposes that in a world devoid of inherent meaning, individuals can find purpose and happiness by fully engaging in the present, accepting the absurdity of existence, and creating their own values. "The Rebel," on the other hand, delves into the nature of rebellion and the complexities of ethics and justice. Camus challenges the dichotomy of absolute morality and advocates for a nuanced understanding of rebellion against oppression. He explores the tension between the individual's desire for personal freedom and the responsibility toward creating a just society.

Camus's unique writing style, characterised by its clarity and conciseness, captivated readers and continues to resonate today. Influenced by existentialism and his experiences growing up in colonial Algeria, Camus crafted narratives that blended his philosophical ideas with compelling storytelling. His ability to infuse philosophical concepts into his works without sacrificing the narrative's flow or undermining the reader's engagement fuelled Camus's literary success.

Beyond his literary achievements, Camus's political engagements also shaped his legacy. His criticism of totalitarianism and his advocacy for individual freedom made him a controversial figure, especially during the tumultuous period of the Algerian War. While Camus initially supported Algerian independence, he opposed the terrorist tactics of the National Liberation Front (FLN). This stance caused a rift between Camus and other prominent intellectuals of the time, including Jean-Paul Sartre, who accused Camus of intellectual and moral failure.

Camus's untimely death in 1960, at the age of 46, in a car accident cut short a career that was still in its prime. However, his works continue to resonate with readers worldwide. Camus's exploration of the human condition, the absurdity of existence, and the resllience of the human spirit remain deeply relevant in today's society. His writings compel us to confront the complexities of morality, the pursuit of meaning, and the delicate balance between personal freedom and the collective responsibility to create a just society.

Albert Camus, the acclaimed writer and philosopher, left an extraordinary legacy. His works invite us to question our existence, embrace the mysteries of life, and find meaning within the absurdity. Join us as we embark on a journey to uncover the life, ideas, and enduring impact of Albert Camus, a writer whose legacy continues to shape and inspire generations.

One

Overview of Albert Camus's Influence in Literature and Existential Philosophy

Albert Camus is considered one of the greatest literary figures of the 20th century, renowned for his profound insights into the human condition and his distinctive writing style. His works continue to captivate and challenge readers with their philosophical depth and introspective exploration.

At the heart of Camus's literary endeavours lies a relentless pursuit of truth and meaning. From his earliest works, such as "The Stranger," to his later essays, "The Myth of Sisyphus," Camus confronts fundamental questions about existence, morality, and the absurdity of life. He invites readers to confront uncomfortable realities through his characters and narratives, encouraging them to question societal norms and conventional wisdom.

"The Stranger," Camus's breakout novel, introduces us to Meursault, a detached and apathetic protagonist who navigates life with an unsettling indifference. As the story unfolds, Meursault's actions and perceptions challenge traditional notions of morality, stirring readers to reassess their own moral compass. Through Meursault, Camus explores the consequences of conformity and the impossible quest for authenticity in a world inherently devoid of objective meaning.

Camus's subsequent work, "The Plague," presents a different facet of his introspective exploration. Set in a city ravaged by a deadly epidemic, the novel delves into themes of isolation, despair, and the human struggle for liberation. Through vividly depicted characters faced with the absurdity of their existence, Camus offers profound insights into the resilience and collective spirit of individuals confronting adversity. "The Plague" becomes an allegory for our existential struggles, reminding us of the human capacity to find hope and meaning in the face of apparent meaninglessness.

In "The Fall," Camus delves even deeper into the complexities of human nature and the dynamics of guilt and judgement. Through monologues delivered by Jean-Baptiste Clamence, a morally conflicted former lawyer, Camus exposes the hypocrisy and contradictions in society and the human psyche. Clamence's introspection unveils the dark recesses of human consciousness, forcing readers to confront their own moral ambiguities and question the authenticity of their actions. It's in this confrontation that Camus invites us to examine our own complicity in perpetuating the very absurdity we wish to escape.

Camus's philosophical contributions extend beyond his literary works and into his essays. In "The Myth of Sisyphus," he introduces the concept of the absurd, asserting that human existence is inherently without inherent meaning or purpose. Rather than succumbing to nihilism or despair, however, Camus proposes that individuals embrace the challenge of creating meaning. By embracing our freedom and accepting the absurdity of life, we can find fulfilment and purpose in even the most apparently meaningless tasks. Camus offers a path to authentic living through this act of rebellion against the absurd.

It is impossible to discuss the impact of Albert Camus without acknowledging his role in shaping existential philosophy as a whole. While he is often associated with absurdism, his contributions to existentialism reach far beyond. His emphasis on embracing personal freedom and responsibility resonated with other philosophers and thinkers of the time, such as Jean-Paul Sartre and Simone de Beauvoir. Camus's ideas fuelled intellectual debates and further enriched the existentialist tradition, leaving an indelible mark on the field.

Albert Camus's influence extends far beyond his immediate contemporaries and the philosophical circles of his time. His works continue to inspire individuals from all walks of life, resonating with their universal struggles and the perennial human quest for meaning and authenticity. In a tumultuous world marked by uncertainty and the relentless pursuit of meaning, Camus's writings serve as a poignant reminder of the power of self-reflection and the importance of navigating the complexities of existence with resilience and purpose.

In conclusion, Albert Camus's legacy as a renowned writer and philosopher is characterised by his unwavering commitment to exploring the depths of the human condition. Through his literary works and philosophical contributions, he confronts us with uncomfortable truths and challenges our preconceived notions of meaning, morality, and the absurdity of life. Camus's enduring influence lies in his ability to provoke readers to confront existential dilemmas and the complexities of their own existence, urging us to embrace the challenge of creating our own meaning in a world too often devoid of it.

Two

Brief Biography and Historical Context of His Life and Work

Albert Camus, a renowned writer and philosopher, was born on November 7, 1913, in Mondovi, a small town in French Algeria. Lucien Camus's father was a poorly educated and frequently unemployed agricultural worker. His mother, Catherine Sintes, of Spanish descent, worked as a cleaning woman and raised Albert and his older brother, Lucien, in difficult circumstances.

Growing up in a working-class neighbourhood, Camus was exposed to the harsh realities of poverty, which left a lasting impression on his writing and philosophy. Despite his challenges, Camus displayed remarkable academic aptitude from a young age. He was awarded a scholarship to attend a prestigious secondary school in Algiers, where he excelled academically and discovered his passion for literature and writing.

However, financial limitations compelled Camus to interrupt his education and take on various odd jobs to assist his family. During this time, he worked as a clerk, a tutor, and even a weatherman before finally being able to return to school and complete his studies. This period of struggle and perseverance profoundly shaped Camus's outlook on poverty, social injustice, and the individual's responsibility to confront and address these issues.

In 1932, Camus earned his baccalaureate in philosophy and enrolled at the University of Algiers. These formative years were immensely influential as Camus delved deeper into literature, philosophy, and theatre. He actively participated in local theatre productions, wrote plays, and contributed to various student publications. During this time, Camus encountered influential figures such as Jean Grenier, his philosophy professor, who nurtured Camus's intellectual curiosity and helped shape his philosophical perspective.

In 1936, tragedy struck when Camus contracted tuberculosis, a devastating disease that forced him to confront his own mortality. This confrontation with his own fragility and the harsh reality of living with illness profoundly impacted Camus's attitude towards life and his philosophical enquiries. His illness became a metaphor for the fundamental question of the human condition - the meaning of existence in the face of an indifferent universe.

During his university years, Camus became affiliated with a group of intellectuals known as "The Absurd," who rejected traditional beliefs, religion, and social norms. Their collective exploration of existential philosophy deepened Camus's understanding of the absurdity of human existence and laid the groundwork for his later works.

In the early 1940s, Camus relocated to Paris, where he joined the French Resistance during World War II. He wrote for underground newspapers and used his writing to express his anti-fascist beliefs and his desire for a free and just society. During this period of intense political engagement, Camus began to solidify his existentialist philosophy and further develop his literary skills.

In 1942, Camus published his first major philosophical work, "The Myth of Sisyphus." This essay explored the concept of the absurd, arguing that human beings are constantly striving for meaning and purpose in a fundamentally meaningless world. Camus famously proclaimed, "There is, but one severe philosophical problem and that is suicide." He emphasised the necessity of acknowledging the absurdity of existence while persisting in pursuing a meaningful and authentic life.

Camus's literary career reached new heights with his novel "The Stranger" publication in 1942. The story follows Meursault, a detached and amoral protagonist who confronts the absurdity of life and society's indifference. Meursault's indifference, both in the face of his mother's death and the moral conventions of the world, sparked intense debates among readers and critics. Through Meursault's journey, Camus explored themes of alienation, isolation, and the struggle to find meaning and purpose in an absurd world.

In 1947, Camus published his allegorical novel "The Plague," set in the fictional town of Oran. This work, considered one of his masterpieces, captures the horrors and moral dilemmas the inhabitants face as they confront an outbreak of the plague. As the town faces an existential crisis, the book delves into questions of morality, human solidarity, and the need for compassion in the face of suffering.

Camus's writing was not confined to fiction and philosophy. He also delved into theatre, producing plays like "Caligula," "The Misunderstanding," and "The Just Assassins." These dramatic works continued to explore existential themes and reflected Camus's ongoing commitment to political activism and social justice.

Throughout his life, Camus maintained a firm stance against totalitarianism and colonialism. However, his position on the Algerian War, which erupted in 1954, drew both praise and criticism. Camus advocated for a peaceful resolution that recognised the rights of both French and Algerians, but this view placed him in a precarious position between French and Algerian nationalists.

Despite his profound impact on literature and philosophy, Camus's life was cut tragically short when he died in a car accident on January 4, 1960, at the age of 46. His death left an irreplaceable void in the world of literature and intellectualism, but his legacy continues to captivate readers and inspire philosophical debates.

In conclusion, Albert Camus's upbringing in poverty, determination to pursue education and writing, battle with illness, and involvement in the French Resistance all played significant roles in shaping his philosophy and literature. His exploration of existential themes, his critique of social injustices, and his unwavering commitment to truth and freedom have established him as an influential figure in the world of literature and philosophy. His works continue to serve as a reminder of the complexities of the human condition and the pursuit of meaning in an often absurd and indifferent world.

Three

Early Life and Formative Years

Albert Camus was born on November 7, 1913, in Mondovi, a small coastal town in French Algeria. The beauty and diversity of the Algerian landscape, with its sandy beaches, lush mountains, and vibrant cities, served as a backdrop to Camus's early life and would later find its way into the vivid descriptions of nature in his writing.

Born into a humble family, Camus's childhood was characterised by the struggles and hardships faced by his family and the community around him. His father, Lucien Camus, who had fought in World War I, died from war-related injuries when Albert was just one year old. With little financial support, Albert and his mother, Catherine, moved to Belcourt, a working-class neighbourhood in Algiers. In this bustling and diverse neighbourhood, Camus would encounter a kaleidoscope of cultures and influences that shaped his understanding of the world.

Catherine, a Spanish-Balearic descent and an illiterate cleaning woman, became a central figure in Camus's life. She raised him with remarkable determination, working multiple jobs to provide for her son. Despite her own hardships, she instilled in him a strong work ethic, resilience, and empathy for others. Through her words and actions, Catherine demonstrated the importance of standing up for justice and treating others with kindness, shaping Camus's moral compass in the process.

Education played a crucial role in Camus's intellectual development. At the local primary school, he displayed exceptional academic talent, impressing his teachers with his intellectual curiosity and passion for learning. Recognising his potential, his teachers encouraged him to pursue his education further. In 1923, Camus was awarded a scholarship to attend the Lycée Bugeaud in Algiers, a renowned French school that would provide him with a solid foundation in literature, philosophy, and critical thinking.

It was during his time at the lycée that Camus's love for literature and philosophy began to bloom. He devoured books from the school library, immersing himself in the works of classical authors such as Homer, Voltaire, and Balzac. These early literary encounters exposed him to different narrative styles and themes and fuelled his ambition to become a writer.

Camus's voracious reading extended beyond the confines of the school curriculum. He ventured into the literary movements of his time, exploring the works of Symbolist poets such as Charles Baudelaire and Arthur Rimbaud, whose lyrical and evocative language influenced his own writing style. Camus also discovered the works of Friedrich Nietzsche, whose bold ideas of individual freedom and the rejection of traditional morality struck a chord with his emerging worldview.

His literary aspirations intertwined with a growing interest in philosophy. Introduced to the discipline by his philosophy teacher, Jean Grenier, Camus delved into philosophical currents that challenged established systems of thought. Camus found himself drawn to existentialism and absurdism as he devoured the works of Jean-Paul Sartre, Martin Heidegger, and Maurice Merleau-Ponty. These philosophical movements explored the inherent meaninglessness of existence and the search for individual meaning in an indifferent universe.

Camus's exposure to these philosophical ideas was not limited to academic exploration. Inspired by the political and social climate of the time, he began to engage actively in political discussions and protests. Algeria, under French colonial rule, was a hotbed of political tensions, and Camus keenly observed the struggles faced by the Algerian people. He joined student debates on the role of colonialism, witnessing both the injustices perpetrated by the French authorities and the tenacity of the Algerian people in their fight for independence.

Camus's growing political awareness led him to embrace communist and anarchist ideologies, which promised a fair and equal society. He saw in these movements the potential to rectify the social and economic disparities he witnessed in his own community. However, as he delved deeper into the ideologies, Camus became increasingly disillusioned with their dogmatic tendencies. He recognised the dangers of fixed ideologies prioritising abstract ideals over individual freedom and personal experience.

Parallel to his academic and political pursuits, Camus also embarked on a writing career in journalism. In 1933, he joined the editorial board of the Alger Républicain, a left-wing newspaper, where he expressed his views on social and political issues, shedding light on the suffering and injustices faced by the working class and marginalised communities. Through his journalism work, Camus experienced the power of the written word as a tool for social change and solidarity.

Life took an unexpected turn for Camus in 1936 when he contracted tuberculosis, a disease that would plague him for the rest of his life. Being confronted with his own mortality at a young age deepened his awareness of the fragility of existence. The experience of fighting against the physical limitations and uncertainty of his own health strengthened Camus's resolve to seize the moments of joy and meaning in life, and this urgency would later permeate his philosophical and literary works.

With their blend of poverty, diversity, intellectual exploration, and personal hardships, Camus's early years in

Algeria left an indelible mark on his writing and worldview. From his humble upbringing and exposure to political injustices, Camus grew to become a voice for the marginalised and a philosopher of the human condition, challenging readers to confront the absurdities and complexities of life. His unique blend of literature and philosophy would later transcend borders and languages, making him one of the most celebrated writers of the 20th century and securing his reputation as a luminary of existentialist thought.

Four

Camus's childhood in Algeria, family background, and early experiences

The renowned French writer and philosopher Albert Camus was born on November 7, 1913, in Mondovi, a small coastal town in French Algeria. The son of Lucien Camus, a hardworking farm labourer, and Catherine Sintès, a diligent house cleaner, Camus's humble upbringing would profoundly influence his literary and philosophical explorations.

Tragically, Camus's father met his untimely demise in 1914 during World War I. This premature loss left young Albert and his older brother, Lucien, under the sole care of their resilient mother. Catherine, fuelled by an unwavering determination, navigated the hardships of single parenthood as she strived to provide her sons with a better future.

Camus's childhood in French Algeria exposed him to the confluence of cultures that characterised the colonial setting. His mother hailed from Spanish ancestry, and his maternal grandmother, a native of Spain, had immigrated to Algeria. This blending of heritages would later infuse Camus's identity and fuel his exploration of themes related to the complexities of identity, colonialism, and social justice.

Camus's mother prioritised education for her sons despite the family's limited means. The young writer attended the local primary school in Mondovi, where his intellectual and creative potential rapidly flourished. His teachers recognised his exceptional talents, often encouraging him to pursue his literary ambitions. It was within the classroom walls that Camus first discovered the power of words and storytelling, igniting a deep passion that would shape his future endeavours.

Subsequently, Camus was granted a scholarship to the prestigious Lycée Bugeaud in Algiers, the capital of Algeria. His time at the Lycée proved transformative, as he excelled academically and delved deeper into his studies of literature and philosophy. Under the guidance of passionate mentors, Camus explored the works of renowned thinkers such as Friedrich Nietzsche, Søren Kierkegaard, and Jean-Paul Sartre. Through rigorous analysis and self-reflection, he began honing his philosophical lens, which would ultimately manifest in his distinctive perspectives on existentialism and the human condition.

During his formative years, Camus encountered personal adversity. At the age of 17, he fell victim to tuberculosis, which forced him to halt his studies temporarily. The confinement and solitude that accompanied his illness provided fertile grounds for introspection. Camus grappled with the inevitability of his own mortality, experiencing firsthand the fragility of human existence. These experiences became the crucible from which his existential outlook would emerge, shaping his philosophical enquiries and literary expressions throughout his life.

In the face of adversities and personal struggles, Camus sought solace in his writing—an art form that became his lifeline. He began contributing essays and articles to local journals and newspapers, showcasing his talent and growing interest in broader societal issues. Through his early works, Camus tantalisingly foreshadowed the themes and ideas that would permeate his later literary and philosophical opuses.

Camus's childhood in French Algeria, enriched by the region's cultural and political tapestry, shaped his worldview. The colonial backdrop, the familial challenges he witnessed, and his own encounters with illness served as catalysts, moulding his profound observations of the human condition. And yet, it was not only the external circumstances that influenced Camus's thoughts but also the inner turmoil he grappled with. His commitment to challenging societal injustices and unravelling existential quandaries became the hallmark of his oeuvre.

As Camus embarked on his journey as a writer and philosopher, he carried with him the myriad influences that sprouted from his upbringing and early experiences. These tenacious roots formed the bedrock of his unique perspective and laid the groundwork for his significant contributions to literature and existential thought. Through his thought-provoking novels, essays, and plays, Camus challenged readers to confront the absurdity of existence while urging them to embrace the fundamental values of compassion, justice, and solidarity. Though his life was tragically cut short in a car accident in 1960 at the age of 46, Albert Camus continues to have a profound impact on readers and thinkers worldwide, leaving behind a remarkable literary legacy that remains as relevant today as it was during his time.

FIVE

EDUCATION AND EARLY EXPOSURE TO PHILOSOPHICAL IDEAS

Camus's upbringing in Algeria significantly shaped his education and exposed him to a wide range of philosophical ideas. Born in Mondovi, Algeria, in 1913, Camus grew up in a working-class family. His father, Lucien Camus, was a poor agricultural worker who died in the Battle of the Marne during World War I. This early loss deeply affected Camus and instilled in him a sense of the fragility of life.

Despite his family's financial hardships, Camus was determined to pursue an education. He attended the University of Algiers, where he studied philosophy and literature. It was during his time at university that he encountered influential thinkers who would have a profound impact on his intellectual development.

One of the most significant influences on Camus was Friedrich Nietzsche. Nietzsche's philosophy of the "will to power" and his critique of traditional morality resonated deeply with Camus, who was drawn to Nietzsche's scepticism towards fixed moral values. Camus was particularly inspired by Nietzsche's concept of the Übermensch or "superman," a figure who creates his own values and embraces the inherent absurdity of life.

In addition to Nietzsche, Camus was also influenced by the pessimistic philosophy of Arthur Schopenhauer. Schopenhauer's belief in the inherent suffering of existence struck a chord with Camus, who had experienced personal tragedy and witnessed Algeria's pervasive poverty and social inequality. This exposure to suffering and injustice would later shape Camus's philosophical exploration of the absurd and his plea for solidarity and empathy.

Søren Kierkegaard, the Danish philosopher known for his existentialist ideas, significantly influenced Camus. Kierkegaard's intense focus on individual existence, subjectivity, and the struggle to attain authentic selfhood deeply resonated with Camus's own existential concerns. Kierkegaard's writings on the anguish of choice and the fear of commitment would find echoes in Camus's works, particularly in his exploration of the moral dilemmas faced by his characters.

While at the university, Camus also became involved in theatrical and political activities. He joined the Social Algerian Revolutionary Party and actively participated in political debates and activities. This engagement heightened his awareness of social issues and the complexities of the human condition. Through his involvement in politics, Camus gained insight into the struggles the marginalised and disenfranchised faced, further shaping his philosophical outlook.

Camus's education was interrupted when he contracted tuberculosis in the early 1930s. Bedridden for long periods, he immersed himself in books and continued his intellectual pursuits. During this convalescence period, he wrote his first philosophical essay, "Christian Metaphysics and Neoplatonism," which explored his early fascination with religion and philosophy.

After recovering from tuberculosis, Camus returned to the University of Algiers to complete his studies. While there, he became involved with the Algerian Communist Party but soon became disillusioned with its ideology. Camus believed in individual freedom and autonomy, which clashed with the party's rigid conformity and disregard for personal liberties. This divide prompted him to distance himself from the party and solidify his own independent philosophical stance.

Camus's education and early exposure to diverse philosophical ideas were crucial in shaping his worldview. The thinkers he encountered and his personal experiences and political engagement laid the foundation for his later philosophical and literary works. Through his exploration of existentialism, the absurd, and the importance of individual freedom, Camus became a prominent figure in philosophical and literary circles, renowned for his penetrating critiques of society and his profound reflections on the human condition.

SIX

THE INFLUENCE OF ALGERIAN CULTURE AND POLITICS ON HIS WORLDVIEW

Camus's childhood in Algeria profoundly influenced his worldview and literary works. Born on November 7, 1913, in Mondovi, French Algeria, he grew up in a modest, working-class family amidst the diverse cultural landscape of his homeland. The rich tapestry of Algerian society, combining French, Arabic, and Berber influences, played a pivotal role in shaping his identity and ideas.

Algeria's tumultuous history of colonisation and the ensuing struggle for independence profoundly impacted Camus's understanding of justice, morality, and the human condition. Growing up in poverty, he was acutely aware of the social and economic disparities between the French colonial ruling class and the marginalised Algerian population. These firsthand experiences ignited a deep-seated sense of empathy, awakening in him a passion for social justice and a commitment to challenging the status quo.

The cultural diversity of Camus's surroundings gave him a unique vantage point in examining the complexities of identity and the clash between different cultures. The amalgamation of French, Arabic, and Berber traditions shaped his understanding of the human experience as something multifaceted and deeply interconnected. It allowed him to explore the tensions that arise when distinct cultures intersect and their profound impact on shaping individuals and societies.

Algeria's political climate further influenced Camus's intellectual development. At a young age, he became politically engaged and joined the Algerian Communist Party in the 1930s. However, as he delved deeper into the theories and practises of communism, he became disillusioned with its deterministic worldview and the suppression of individual freedoms. Subsequently, Camus distanced himself from communist ideologies and instead gravitated towards anarchist and libertarian socialist ideas, emphasising the importance of individual freedom and autonomous decision-making within a just society.

Yet, Camus's complex relationship with Algeria extended beyond his political leanings. As the nationalist movement in Algeria gained momentum, particularly during the 1950s and 1960s, Camus found himself caught between competing loyalties and conflicting accusations.

Some accused him of insufficiently supporting Algerian independence, viewing his advocacy for a peaceful resolution as inadequate. Conversely, others criticised him for his perceived betrayal of his French identity. This delicate balancing act placed significant strain on Camus, who ultimately sought a path towards reconciliation and understanding between opposing factions, envisioning an Algeria that respected both the indigenous population's rights and the French settlers' contributions.

The experiences and observations garnered from his formative years in Algeria instilled in Camus a burning desire to be a compassionate observer of the human condition. He was acutely aware of the contradictions and complexities inherent in colonial rule, igniting a sense of moral outrage that propelled him to challenge social injustices through his writing. The multitude of perspectives and the interplay of cultures he encountered in Algeria sharpened his ability to analyse the human experience, allowing him to delve into existential questions, explore the absurdity of life, and delve into the moral dilemmas faced by individuals in an unjust society.

Camus's Algerian upbringing, with its socio-political tensions and intricate cultural fusion, provided him with a unique lens through which to view and dissect the world. It affirmed his belief that literature and art could be powerful tools for social change and understanding. Algeria, as both a physical and emotional landscape, moulded him into a writer committed to unveiling truth, awakening empathy, and advocating for the pursuit of justice. It is within this crucible of experiences that the literary genius of Albert Camus was forged, leaving an indelible mark in the realm of literature and philosophy.

SEVEN

CAMUS'S PHILOSOPHICAL JOURNEY

Transitioning from journalism to literary and philosophical writing marked a significant turning point in Albert Camus's career. While initially gaining recognition as a journalist, he soon undertook a more profound exploration of philosophical ideas, developing his unique philosophical framework. This extended chapter delves deeper into Camus's early philosophical essays and articles, as well as his involvement in the French Resistance and how it influenced his philosophical outlook.

Camus's philosophical journey began with exploring existential themes, which emerged in his early writings. Influenced by Friedrich Nietzsche, Søren Kierkegaard, and Jean-Paul Sartre, Camus delved into questions surrounding the human condition and the meaning of life. These thinkers gave him a foundation from which he further developed his philosophical thought.

In his essay "The Myth of Sisyphus," Camus critically examined the absurdity of human existence. He found himself captivated by the storey of Sisyphus, a figure condemned by the gods to eternally roll a rock up a hill, only for it to roll back down, necessitating the perpetuation of his futile and exhausting task. Camus saw Sisyphus as an allegory for the human condition, wherein individuals are compelled to find purpose and meaning in a world that does not provide inherent answers.

Drawing from Sartre's existentialist ideas, Camus expanded on the concept of individual freedom and the responsibility that accompanies it. He argued that humans are free to create their own meaning and rebel against the meaninglessness of existence. This idea laid the foundation for his philosophy of absurdism, which suggests that the search for an ultimate truth or meaning is fundamentally futile in an indifferent universe. Rather than despairing in the face of this absurdity, Camus advocated for embracing it and finding personal significance through acts of rebellion and defiance against the absurdity of existence. He believed acknowledging and accepting this absurdity could lead to a liberated and authentic life.

During World War II, Camus actively participated in the French Resistance against the Nazi occupation, an experience that deeply influenced his philosophical outlook. The moral dilemmas faced by Resistance members forced Camus to confront questions of ethics, justice, and individual responsibility. The struggle against oppression and the fight for freedom played a significant role in shaping his philosophical ideas.

Camus's involvement in the Resistance also acquainted him with the fragility and preciousness of human life. Witnessing firsthand the horrors and injustices of war, he became acutely aware of the potential for human suffering and the constant presence of existential anxiety. These experiences fuelled his exploration of the human condition, influencing his later works, including "The Plague."

"The Plague" portrayed a fictional town struck by a deadly epidemic, serving as an allegory for the Nazi occupation of France. Through this novel, Camus further examined the themes of human suffering, the meaning of life in the face of adversity, and the moral obligations that arise during times of crisis. He highlighted the importance of maintaining one's humanity and solidarity with others amid tragedy and chaos.

In "The Rebel," Camus went beyond the themes of absurdism and introduced the concept of rebellion as a response to the world's injustices. He critiqued revolutionary violence and submission to oppressive systems, arguing for a middle ground, emphasising moral integrity and refusing to accept injustices. Camus believed in the power of individual action to effect meaningful change and stressed the importance of compassion and solidarity in building a more just society.

Throughout his philosophical journey, Camus defied categorisation, remaining critical of philosophical and political dogmatism. While associated with the existentialist movement, he forged his own path, avoiding strict adherence to any specific school of thought. He believed in the importance of individual autonomy and intellectual independence, always interrogating prevailing ideas and ideologies.

In conclusion, Camus's philosophical journey marked a transformative phase in his literary career. Camus forged a unique philosophical framework that resonates even today by grappling with existential themes, wrestling with questions of absurdity, and reflecting on his experiences in the French Resistance. His exploration of absurdism, rebellion, freedom, and individual responsibility continues to captivate readers and stimulate profound philosophical discussions. Camus's legacy lies in his literary contributions and the timeless and thought-provoking concepts he introduced to the philosophical discourse, making his journey an indelible and enduring contribution to the intellectual landscape.

EIGHT

TRANSITION FROM JOURNALISM TO LITERARY AND PHILOSOPHICAL WRITING

Albert Camus, widely regarded as one of the most influential writers of the 20th century, embarked on a remarkable journey that propelled him from the world of journalism to the realm of literary and philosophical greatness. Born in Mondovi, Algeria, in 1913, Camus discovered his passion for writing at an early age. As a young man, he immersed himself in the vibrant cultural and intellectual atmosphere of Algiers, where he first explored his talents as a journalist.

Camus's foray into journalism began in his early twenties when he became involved with a local theatre group. This involvement led to his eventual appointment as the theatre critic for the newspaper "Alger républicain." Within these pages, his eloquent and insightful critiques captivated readers, revealing his ability to dissect and analyse art in a way that transcended mere opinion. This early experience honed his skills in observation and articulation, laying the groundwork for his captivating literary and philosophical works to come.

However, Camus's journey as a journalist was not without its challenges. In Algeria, a colony of France, the political and social landscape was marked by inequality and oppression. The Algerian people resisted the colonial rule, and Camus, a white Frenchman, was torn between different worlds. He was sympathetic to the struggles of the Algerian people, but as a journalist, he also had to reckon with the complexities of his own identity and position. Although initially drawn to journalism by his love for theatre and culture, Camus soon realised that literature and philosophy offered him the tools to delve deeper into the human condition and tackle the world's pressing issues.

During his time as a journalist, Camus encountered the harsh realities of his native Algeria. The region was a crucible of colonial exploitation, where racial discrimination and economic hardship were a daily reality for the Algerian people. These experiences deeply impacted Camus, awakening his sense of social justice and the desire to bring change through his writing. The power of journalism lies in its ability to shed light on hidden truths, expose injustice, and weave narratives that resonate with the masses. Camus saw the potential of his craft to incite collective action, mobilise public opinion, and expose the contradictions of the colonial system.

Camus's journey took an unexpected turn during World War II when he joined the French Resistance, an underground movement committed to fighting against the Nazi occupation. This period of intense political engagement further solidified his commitment to using writing as a tool for justice and resistance. As a member of "Combat," an underground newspaper, Camus fearlessly penned articles and editorials, championing the cause of freedom while unmasking the hypocrisy and cruelty of the occupying regime. At great risk to his own safety, Camus used his words as a weapon, contributing to the resistance effort and inspiring countless others to join the fight for liberty. While his journalistic contributions were undoubtedly impactful, Camus yearned for a more profound and lasting means of expression—one that would transcend the ephemeral nature of newspaper reporting.

During this transformative period, Camus began to embrace literature as a medium for exploring existential themes and the complexity of human existence. He believed that the power of storytelling could illuminate the depths of the human condition and provoke readers to confront their own sense of purpose and meaning in an indifferent world. Leaving behind the transitory urgency of journalism, Camus set forth on a new creative path that would shape his legacy.

In 1942, Camus's debut novel, "The Stranger," was published, capturing the attention of readers and firmly establishing his reputation as a significant literary voice. The enigmatic protagonist, Meursault, embodying the philosophy of the absurd, questions the fundamental assumptions of society and confronts the existential void. Through Meursault's detachment and indifference, Camus artfully revealed the banality and unpredictability of life, challenging conventional notions of meaning and purpose.

With the success of "The Stranger," Camus continued to explore profound existential themes in his subsequent works. In 1947, he published "The Plague," a haunting and powerful novel that metaphorically addressed the horrors of war and the human capacity for resilience in the face of adversity. Set in the fictional town of Oran, the story follows the inhabitants as they grapple with a mysterious and deadly plague, metaphorically representing the universal struggle against suffering and the fragility of human existence. Through evocative prose and vivid characterisation, Camus delved into questions of morality, freedom, and the nature of heroism.

Camus's transition from journalism to literary and philosophical writing was not merely a shift in career but a profound metamorphosis that allowed him to explore the depths of his inherent philosophical ideas. In his works, he wrestled with the human condition's contradictions, absurdities, and moral ambiguities. Drawing on his observations as a journalist, Camus transformed reality into art, inviting readers to introspect, question, and find meaning within their own lives.

His literary works became vehicles for his philosophical ideas, breathing life into abstract concepts and making them accessible to a broader audience. Through characters such as Meursault and the inhabitants of Oran, Camus illuminated the complexities of the human psyche while gently prodding his readers to search for authenticity and confront the fundamental questions of existence. Through his novels, plays, or philosophical essays, Camus became known for blending literature and philosophy, challenging conventional boundaries and establishing a lasting legacy.

Camus's journey from journalism to literary and philosophical greatness was self-discovery and profound introspection. Through the power of storytelling, he transcended the limitations of journalism and harnessed the written word to provoke thought and awaken conscience. Camus ventured deeper into the human experience with each written work, fearlessly exposing the contradictions, injustices, and absurdities that define our existence. His contribution to literature and philosophy solidified his reputation as a renowned writer. It sparked a revolution of thought, inviting individuals to confront the inherent complexities of the human condition and forge their own paths in the face of an uncertain and indifferent world.

NINE

EXPLORATION OF CAMUS'S EARLY PHILOSOPHICAL ESSAYS AND ARTICLES

In this chapter, we will explore Albert Camus's early philosophical essays and articles that influenced his intellectual growth and formed the basis of his later work. During his developmental years, Camus actively delved into philosophical concepts and pondered the significance of life and human existence. This phase of intellectual exploration sets the stage for comprehending the significant influence Camus would go on to wield in the realms of literature and philosophy.

One of Camus's significant early works is his essay "The Myth of Sisyphus," published in 1942. In this essay, Camus introduces the concept of absurdism, which became central to his philosophy. He argues that the human condition is inherently meaningless and absurd and that the search for absolute meaning is ultimately futile. Camus presents the mythological figure of Sisyphus, condemned to eternally roll a boulder uphill only for it to roll back down, as a metaphor for the absurd struggle of human existence. Through this profound allegory, Camus provokes readers to question the purpose and significance of their lives, urging them to embrace the absurdity rather than despair in the face of an inherently indifferent universe.

Camus's exploration of the absurd is further complemented by his collection of essays titled "The Rebel," published in 1951. In this work, Camus delves into the concept of rebellion and its significance in the face of an absurd world. He explores the nature of rebellion against oppressive systems and ideologies, advocating for a rebellion rooted in individual autonomy and refusal to accept unjust conditions. Camus challenges the notions of absolute revolution and explores the complexities of rebellion as a moral and philosophical act. Through this exploration, he highlights the importance of maintaining one's integrity and authenticity in the face of adversity and the duty of individuals to live an ethical life despite the inherent absurdity of existence.

During his early years, Camus was also influenced by existentialist thought, particularly the writings of Jean-Paul Sartre and Simone de Beauvoir. However, he eventually diverged from existentialism and developed his own distinct philosophy. While existentialism emphasises individual freedom and choice, Camus's philosophy places greater emphasis on the human condition and the inevitable tension between our desire for meaning and the inherent absurdity of existence. He explores the notion that while life may lack inherent meaning, it is up to individuals to create their own meaning and engage in acts of rebellion and solidarity to combat the absurdity.

Camus's early philosophical essays and articles reveal the depth of his intellectual enquiry and refine his philosophical ideas further. For example, his essay "The Artist and His Time" explores the role of the artist in society and the potential for artistic creation to be a form of rebellion against the absurd. Camus argues that artists, through their art, can challenge the status quo and offer alternatives to prevailing social, political, and cultural paradigms. He emphasises the need for artists to remain true to their vision and avoid compromising their integrity for fame or societal approval.

In addition to these philosophical essays, Camus was also a prolific journalist and writer of articles. Through his journalistic work, he explored political and social issues of his time, often offering insightful commentary and critique. For instance, his writings on colonialism and the Algerian War reflect his deep commitment to justice and human rights. Camus used his platform as a writer to shed light on the atrocities committed under colonial rule and to advocate for the rights of colonised people. His unwavering dedication to addressing societal injustices underscores his belief in the power of literature and intellectual discourse to effect meaningful change.

Camus's early philosophical essays and articles showcased his intellectual prowess and played a crucial role in shaping his worldview and mature philosophical ideas. They set the stage for his later novels and plays, where he would further explore themes of absurdity, rebellion, and the complexities of human nature. The significance of these early works cannot be overstated, as they laid the groundwork for Camus's enduring impact on literature and existential philosophy. The profound insights and thought-provoking arguments presented in these essays continue to resonate with readers, urging them to question the nature of existence and confront the inherent absurdity of life.

Thus, we gain a deeper understanding of his intellectual journey and the evolution of his ideas through Camus's early philosophical essays and articles. These works illuminate his exploration of existential questions and his unwavering commitment to justice and humanity. Camus's writings inspire readers worldwide, inviting them to reflect deeply on the meaning and purpose of their individual lives and the collective human experience. As we delve deeper into Camus's literary and philosophical legacy, we begin to grasp this renowned writer and philosopher's enduring relevance and timeless insights.

Ten

Examination of his role in the French Resistance and its influence on his work

Albert Camus's involvement in the French Resistance during World War II profoundly impacted his personal life and literary works. As a writer, Camus was known for his ability to tackle complex philosophical questions and explore the human condition. However, the period of his involvement in the Resistance further deepened his understanding of these themes and added layers of meaning to his writing.

In 1940, following the German occupation of France, Camus initially joined the French Communist Party. However, disillusioned by the party's alignment with Soviet policies, he left after only a year. He then turned his attention to journalism, believing that public opinion and awareness were essential in opposing the Nazi regime.

Camus officially joined the Resistance in 1943, demonstrating his unwavering commitment to fight against the oppressors who had taken over his homeland. This decision was not made lightly, as he was well aware of the risks and dangers involved in defying the Nazis. However, he believed freedom and justice were worth fighting for and felt morally obligated to stand up against the oppressive regime.

Working as a journalist for the underground newspaper Combat, Camus used his writing skills to contribute to the resistance efforts. He risked his life by writing articles denouncing the occupation and encouraging resistance. These articles were often clandestinely distributed, providing hope and inspiration to those fighting for freedom.

Camus's time in the Resistance exposed him to the harsh realities of war and oppression. He witnessed firsthand the atrocities committed by the Nazis and the immense suffering endured by those under their rule. These experiences deepened Camus's understanding of human nature and the capacity for great evil and unwavering resistance.

In addition to his journalistic contributions, Camus participated in acts of armed resistance. He worked as a courier, transporting coded messages and documents between different cells of the Resistance. His work required efficiency, resourcefulness, and a keen sense of vigilance.

The constant threat of discovery hung over him, yet he maintained his determination to resist the occupation until the liberation of France.

It was during this tumultuous period that Camus's existentialist philosophy took shape. The absurdity of war and the realisation of humanity's capacity for destruction prompted him to critically examine the meaning and purpose of human existence. In one of his letters, Camus wrote, "I had discovered at that moment that I was marked by the absurd, that I was bearing it within me as a curse."

Camus's experiences in the underground movement and encounters with individuals from different walks of life profoundly affected the themes and characters in his novels and plays. The profound psychological impact of war can be witnessed in his masterpiece, "The Stranger." Its protagonist, Meursault, is characterised by his indifference and detachment from the world around him, which can be interpreted as a response to the absurdity and horrors of war. Meursault's existential crisis and eventual rebellion against societal norms mirror Camus's own struggle to find meaning and purpose in a world gripped by chaos and violence.

Similarly, in "The Plague," Camus explores the existential struggle of individuals in the face of an epidemic that can be seen as an allegory for the Nazi occupation. The residents of the fictional town of Oran are forced to confront their own mortality and the lack of control they have over their lives. Through their collective efforts to combat the plague, Camus underscores the importance of solidarity, resilience, and resistance against suffering.

Camus's work "The Rebel" is perhaps his most direct exploration of the themes of resistance and morality. In this book, he delves deep into the concept of rebellion and examines how individuals can retain their integrity and dignity in the face of oppressive systems. Drawing on his experiences in the Resistance, Camus critiques totalitarian regimes and nihilistic responses to oppression, asserting that true rebellion lies in affirming human dignity and combating injustice.

Furthermore, the themes of freedom, justice, and the struggle for autonomy can also be found in many of Camus's other works. "The Fall" examines the moral guilt that individuals carry and the hypocrisy of society. "Caligula" delves into the corrupting influences of power and the consequences of unchecked authority. Through these works, Camus challenges readers to confront the contradictions and complexities of human existence, urging them to choose rebellion against dehumanising forces.

Camus's involvement in the Resistance shaped his writing and his post-war political engagements. He continued to use his platform to advocate for justice, equality, and human rights. Despite the controversies and disagreements surrounding his political views, Camus remained committed to the idea of preserving human dignity in the face of oppression.

In conclusion, Albert Camus's role in the French Resistance profoundly influenced his literary works. It shaped his understanding of existential questions, his exploration of rebellion and resilience, and his commitment to justice and human rights. His experiences during this period added depth and authenticity to his writings, continuing to resonate with readers and inspiring meaningful reflections on the human condition. Through his brave actions and profound insights, Camus demonstrated the power of art to provoke reflection, ignite change, and ultimately affirm the inherent value of human life.

Eleven

Major Works and Themes

One of Albert Camus's most celebrated works is "The Stranger" (also known as "The Outsider"). Published in 1942, this philosophical novel tells the story of Meursault, an emotionally detached protagonist caught up in a senseless murder. Through Meursault's dispassionate narration of his trial and subsequent execution, Camus examines the theme of absurdity and its implications for the human condition. Meursault's indifference to societal norms, his refusal to satisfy conventional moral expectations, and his relentless honesty reveal the gulf between individual consciousness and the expectations of society. The novel's existential underpinnings challenge traditional notions of morality, rationality, and the search for meaning, leaving readers to ponder the fundamental question: can we find meaning, purpose, or justice in a fundamentally meaningless and indifferent universe?

Another monumental work by Camus is "The Plague" (1947), a novel set in the fictional Algerian town of Oran. It serves as both an allegory for the Nazi occupation of France during World War II and a profound exploration of the human condition. Through the relentless outbreak of an insidious plague in Oran, Camus delves into the nature of human suffering, the precariousness of life, and the absurdity of existence. The plague becomes a metaphor for humanity's complex struggles, and how individuals respond to it reflects their moral character and attempts to find meaning in an irrational world. "The Plague" raises profound questions about morality, heroism, and individuals' choices in extreme circumstances. It is a powerful reflection on the nature of human resilience and the eternal struggle between life and death.

Camus's philosophical essay, "The Myth of Sisyphus" (1942), remains a cornerstone of existential thought. Inspired by the Greek mythological figure Sisyphus, who is condemned to eternally roll a boulder up a hill, only to have it roll back down, Camus examines the human experience of absurdity. He argues that life is inherently absurd, devoid of any predetermined meaning or purpose. The essay contemplates the tension between the human desire for meaning and the inherent meaninglessness of the universe. Camus suggests that the only valid response to this absurdity is not despair or nihilism but rather a conscious rebellion against the absurd. He proposes that individuals must embrace the struggle, create their own meaning, and find fulfilment in the act of rebellion.

In "The Fall" (1956), Camus presents a character study through the narration of Jean-Baptiste Clamence, a former lawyer in Amsterdam. Clamence confesses his sins and moral failures to an unidentified listener, offering a candid examination of his own guilt and hypocrisy. This introspective monologue delves into the human inclination to judge others while evading self-reflection, exposing the fallibility of morality and the contradictions inherent in human existence. "The Fall" raises profound questions about the nature of responsibility, honesty, and the complexities of the human condition.

Camus's exploration of these major works showcases his consistent examination of themes such as absurdity, existentialism, and the human condition. He challenges readers to confront the complexities of human existence, the absence of inherent meaning, and the necessity for individuals to take responsibility for their own lives.

Beyond these major works, Camus also developed his philosophical beliefs through essays, plays, and journalism. His essays, such as "The Rebel" and "The Crisis of Man," further explored the themes of revolt, freedom, and the individual's societal role. Camus's plays, including "Caligula" and "The Misunderstanding," grappled with existential questions within dramatic settings. Furthermore, his journalistic writings, collected in books like "Resistance, Rebellion, and Death," reflected his political activism, championing justice, human rights, and the resistance against oppressive regimes.

Camus's literary and philosophical contributions continue to resonate in the contemporary world, inspiring readers and thinkers to contemplate the fundamental questions of existence, responsibility, and the pursuit of meaning amidst the complexities of life. By challenging established beliefs, Camus invites readers to critically examine their own lives and forge their own paths, embracing a philosophy of authenticity and moral integrity. His ideas remind us of the importance of personal agency and the eternal struggle to find purpose and fulfilment in an absurd world.

TWELVE

IN-DEPTH ANALYSIS OF "THE STRANGER" AND THE THEME OF ABSURDITY

"The Stranger" is one of the most profound and enigmatic works ever gracing the literary canon. Albert Camus, the brilliant architect of this existential masterpiece, flawlessly captures the essence of the absurdity and meaninglessness that permeate the human experience. In this extended analysis, we will dive even deeper into the intricate layers of this novel, unveiling its profound philosophical underpinnings and illuminating the profound implications it holds for our understanding of existence.

At its core, "The Stranger" strobes like a beacon, challenging long-standing notions of rationality and the relentless quest for meaning. Through its protagonist,

Meursault, Camus offers a scintillating exploration of the absurdities that course through our lives, unceasingly mocking our long-established certainties and aspirations. Meursault's character emerges as a profound symbol of this absurdity, as he resists conforming to societal expectations, defiantly rejecting conventional interpretations of emotion and morality. Through his detached and indifferent disposition, Camus beckons readers to question the foundations upon which our beliefs and actions are constructed.

The novel's opening chapters expose us to Meursault's life, which seems to unfold in the desolate embrace of purposelessness. His monotonous daily routine mirrors the banality of human existence, embodying the existential ennui that relentlessly besieges the hearts and minds of countless individuals. Camus, a literary architect of unparalleled brilliance, masterfully employs this seemingly mundane backdrop to accentuate the absurdity that pervades our existence, pointing to the futility of our endeavours and aspirations amidst an indifferent universe.

The death of Meursault's mother arrives as a pivotal moment within the narrative, serving as a vivid reminder of the central theme of absurdity. Rather than surrendering to the conventional waves of grief and engaging in customary mourning rituals, Meursault remains detached, focusing instead on the raw and immediate sensory experiences that envelop him. This unyielding rejection of societal norms immediately unsettles those around him, exposing the bewildering arbitrariness that governs their expectations. Camus impels readers to recognise the absurdity inherent in mourning a person who no longer exists, urging them to question the necessity of such rigid displays of emotion.

As Meursault becomes embroiled in a web of events that ultimately culminate in a senseless act of violence, Camus skillfully peels back the layers of human behaviour and judgement, further exposing their irrationality. The subsequent trial, which initially appears to be an enquiry into the murder itself, subtly and intricately transforms into a spectacle that lays bare society's relentless condemnation of Meursault's indifference and refusal to conform to its moral codes. In presenting the courtroom proceedings as a futile quest for retributive justice, Camus reveals the inherent absurdity of attempting to impose order and reason upon a chaotic and unpredictable world.

Through the lens of existentialism, "The Stranger" challenges readers to confront the profound question of the search for meaning in an indifferent universe. With his unwavering acceptance of the absurdity that underlies existence, Meursault emerges as the embodiment of the absurd hero, one who confronts the contradictions and uncertainties of life without flinching, refusing to surrender to the grip of despair. Camus's magnum opus demands that readers question their own assumptions and preconceived notions about the nature of reality. By dismantling conventional categorisations of morality and rationality, the author invites us to reassess the fragile systems of meaning we construct for ourselves, confront the arbitrary nature of our beliefs and embrace the complexities and paradoxes that define the human condition.

"The Stranger" serves as both a profound reminder of the pervasive absurdities that lurk beneath the surface of our existence and a poignant invitation to embrace the enigmatic complexities of life. Through its pages, Camus awakens a heightened awareness of our own existential dilemmas, relentlessly urging us to confront the inherent incongruities and uncertainties that define our journey. This literary masterpiece seizes our consciousness, leaving an indelible imprint that resonates long after reluctantly turning the final page.

Thirteen

Exploration of "The Plague" as a Reflection on Human Nature and Morality

"The Plague" is a timeless masterpiece of existential literature penned by the renowned French-Algerian writer. This profound novel explores the depths of human nature, delving into complex themes of morality, suffering, and the relentless search for meaning in an absurd world. The fiction is set in the town of Oran; the story unfolds against the backdrop of a devastating plague that gradually consumes the lives of its inhabitants, forcing them to confront their deepest fears, desires, and inherent mysteries of existence.

Camus skillfully employs the plague as a powerful metaphor, encapsulating individuals' existential struggle in their quest for purpose and understanding in life. Like a malevolent wake-up call, the sudden outbreak rudely interrupts the townspeople's mundane routines and complacent lives, ripping through the fabric of their existence and unmasking the harsh, underlying reality of their mortality. In the face of this relentless plague, ordinary individuals find themselves forced to grapple with the inevitability of suffering, the inevitability of death, and the crushing weight of uncertainty that so often accompanies the human experience.

Through his masterful depiction of characters, Camus paints a vivid snapshot of the diverse responses elicited by the plague, offering profound insights into the complexity and contradictions of human nature. Among the tapestry of personalities, Dr Bernard Rieux emerges as a symbol of unwavering solidarity and compassion—a beacon of hope amidst the darkness that engulfs Oran. Tirelessly working to combat the disease, he acts as a moral compass, offering relief to the afflicted and solace to the suffering. Through his unwavering determination and selfless actions, we witness the indomitable strength of the human spirit when facing overwhelming adversity.

Equally fascinating is the enigmatic figure of Jean Tarrou. Tarrou, a stranger in Oran, epitomises Camus' exploration of morality, questioning the nature of ethical choices in an absurd world. His profound insights and unwavering commitment to capturing fleeting moments of empathy and understanding challenge the townspeople to confront their own prejudices, selfishness, and shortcomings. Tarrou's intellectual and moral depth is a beacon of hope and inspiration amidst the moral decay that has beset the town. In this, Camus presents a poignant critique of a society absorbed by its own selfish desires and blind to the suffering of others.

However, even as Rieux and Tarrou represent the best of humanity in the face of crisis, Camus does not shy away from exposing the darker aspects of human nature. The plague, acting as a magnifying glass, reveals the capacity for moral degradation amid chaos. The townspeople, overwhelmed by fear and self-interest, experience an erosion of morality, becoming entangled in acts of selfishness, indifference, and even profiteering from the misfortune of others. These characters are stark reminders of the fragility and complexity of moral choices, highlighting the delicate tightrope individuals and society walk during times of existential crisis.

Throughout the narrative, Camus raises crucial ethical questions, forcing readers to confront the very nature of morality itself. Does morality possess universal principles, or are those principles fluid and mutable, altering according to the exigencies of our circumstances? The relentless plague rips societal norms apart, exposing the frailties and contradictions within individuals and society, thus prompting readers to reassess their moral frameworks and reflect upon the consequences of their choices.

In conclusion, in its timeless brilliance, Albert Camus' "The Plague" delves fervently into the recesses of human nature and morality. The gripping tale sheds light on individuals' profound struggles in the face of suffering, despair, and the ever-pervasive spectre of mortality. It serves as a potent reminder of life's inherent fragility and uncertainty, compelling readers to confront their own moral choices, wrestle with the essence of their existence, and navigate the journey for meaning in a world that often appears marred by absurdity and devoid of inherent purpose.

FOURTEEN

DISCUSSION OF "THE MYTH OF SISYPHUS" AND CAMUS'S CONCEPT OF ABSURDISM

"The Myth of Sisyphus" stands as one of the most influential philosophical essays of the 20th century, plunging into the depths of existentialism and the nature of the human condition. In this chapter, we delve further into Albert Camus's exploration of absurdism as he masterfully analyses the mythological figure Sisyphus in a profound and thought-provoking manner.

Camus's journey into philosophical enquiry begins with an essential question that has haunted humankind for centuries: Is life worth living in the face of its fundamental absurdity? He asserts that within the human condition lies a profound discord, an inherent conflict between our innate desire for meaning, purpose, and order and the chaotic, meaningless nature of the universe. This existential tension forms the very crux of Camus's concept of absurdism.

In his examination of the myth of Sisyphus, Camus skillfully draws parallels between Sisyphus's eternal struggle and the plight of humanity. According to Greek mythology, Sisyphus was condemned by the gods to an eternity of fruitlessly rolling a boulder uphill, only to witness it tragically roll back down, compelling him to resume the laborious task eternally—an unending cycle of futility. Camus posits that individuals are trapped in a similar predicament, tirelessly pursuing meaning and purpose while grappling with the universe's ultimate indifference.

However, Camus does not view this absurdity as a cause for despair or nihilism. Instead, he proposes that humans must confront the absurdity of existence head-on, bravely accepting and defying its grip. This conscious acceptance and rebellion against the absurd, Camus argues, is the only means of true liberation. By directly engaging with the absurd, individuals can discover a profound sense of freedom and authenticity that transcends the illogical and meaningless nature of the world.

Additionally, Camus posits rebellion as a central pathway to breaking free from the chains of absurdity. In this regard, Sisyphus becomes an archetypal figure, embodying humanity's universal struggle against forces that seek to confine and dictate our lives. Despite his task's perpetual and futile nature, according to Camus, Sisyphus can find solace, happiness, and meaning by fully embracing his fate.

Through accepting the absurd reality and deriving purpose from the endless repetition of his endeavour, Sisyphus defies the whims of the gods and obtains a sense of personal fulfilment.

Through "The Myth of Sisyphus," Camus provocatively challenges and deconstructs traditional notions of meaning and purpose. He dismisses the idea of a transcendent or objective purpose imposed upon humanity, instead emphasising the profound significance of subjective meaning, personally constructed and chosen. For Camus, the meaning becomes an individual responsibility—an empowering act of rebellion against the absurdity of existence. His philosophy of absurdism continues to inspire and ignite philosophical discussions on the nature of life, the complexities of the human condition, and the profound role of rebellion in the face of absurdity.

"The Myth of Sisyphus", "The Stranger", and "The Plague" are eloquent masterpieces that build upon and expand Camus's concept of absurdism, casting a poignant light on the pervasive influence of his philosophical ideas within the realms of literature and existential thought. With their unique blend of introspection, social commentary, and literary prowess, Camus's writings resonate deeply with readers across generations, inviting them to contemplate the intricacies of existence and forge their own meanings amidst the absurdity of life.

FIFTEEN

EXAMINATION OF "THE FALL" AND THEMES OF GUILT AND JUDGMENT

"The Fall" is a remarkable and haunting masterpiece by Albert Camus, delving deep into the realms of guilt and judgement. Set within the confines of an Amsterdam bar, this enigmatic novel takes the form of a mesmerising monologue delivered by the troubled protagonist, Jean-Baptiste Clamence. Through his introspective narrative, Camus skillfully unveils the intricate layers of guilt, remorse, and the elusive pursuit of redemption that torment the human psyche.

Clamence, once a prominent and successful lawyer, is burdened by the weight of his past deeds and the moral compromises he made throughout his career. As the story unravels, readers are captivated by Clamence's passionate self-condemnation, a reflection of his existential guilt—a visceral awareness of his own actions and their profound consequences. The bar in which Clamence compulsively shares his confessions symbolises the deceptively comforting refuge of isolation—a place where one can wallow in one's own self-destruction and grapple with the complexities of one's own guilt.

Within the confines of the Amsterdam bar, Clamence's monologue becomes a confessional, an attempt to untangle the complexities of his own moral fabric. He recounts his experiences as a defence lawyer, where he cleverly manipulated the truth, bending it to fit the narrative that suited his clients. In his pursuit of success and a larger-than-life reputation, he became blinded by his own moral compromises and forgot the weight of his ethical responsibility. But as the facade of his glory crumbled, Clamence's self-awareness was ignited, and guilt seeped into his very core.

Camus masterfully strips away the conventional facade of black and white, plunging readers into the murky depths where moral absolutes crumble at the touch of human frailty. Through Clamence's confessions, readers become aware of the subjectivity of judgement and the complexity of human motives. In his monologue, he exposes the flaws of a hypocritical society that too often condemns others while neglecting to examine its own failings. The bar becomes a microcosm for the world, where the human condition is bared, stripped of its disguises, and examined under the unflinching gaze of Clamence's introspection.

As Clamence wrestles with his own judgements, a profound candidness emerges—a recognition that no one is immune from the allure of deceit and the gripping tendrils of guilt. The fallibility of human nature lies at the heart of his narrative, highlighting a universal truth often suppressed in the pursuit of perfection. Through this self-reflection, Camus implores us to confront our moral dilemmas and acknowledge the shades of grey that permeate our existence. He encourages us to delve into the depths of our consciousness, challenge our preconceived notions, and navigate the labyrinthine complexities of human nature with humility and empathy.

"The Fall" penetrates the depths of the human psyche, urging us to scrutinise our souls and acknowledge our existence's multifaceted nature. Clamence's revelations become a catalyst for self-examination, challenging readers to confront their own shadows and grapple with the true meaning of guilt, judgment, and redemption. In Camus's world, redemption is not attained through grand gestures or hollow promises but through the stark and honest realisation of our own fallibility. Through this acceptance, we gain the capacity to extend compassion, empathy, and forgiveness not only to others but also to ourselves.

With its profound exploration of guilt, judgement, and the complexity of human nature, "The Fall" is a testament to Camus's keen insight into the human condition. It challenges us to confront our own shadows and embrace the ambiguity that lies within. As readers, we are left haunted by the lingering questions, forever contemplating our own capacity for moral judgement and the delicate dance between guilt and redemption that shapes our lives. The bar in Amsterdam becomes more than just a setting; it becomes a mirror reflecting our introspection, urging us to confront our demons within its dimly lit confines.

SIXTEEN

CAMUS'S PHILOSOPHY AND WORLDVIEW

Through his works, Camus delves into the complexities of existence, grappling with the fundamental questions of meaning, purpose, freedom, and the human condition. His exploration of absurdism, existentialism, and humanism offers a rich tapestry of insights into the nature of reality.

At the heart of Camus's philosophy is absurdism, a perspective that challenges the traditional search for an objective meaning or purpose in life. He contends that the universe, with its inherent lack of meaning, confronts humanity with a profound sense of the absurd. This confrontation often leads individuals to question the essence of their existence and may result in despair, nihilism, or existential anguish.

However, Camus does not succumb to the despair of the absurd; rather, he embraces the human struggle to find meaning in an indifferent universe. He argues that despite the absence of inherent meaning, individuals can create their own significance and rebel against existence's inherent meaninglessness. Through this act of rebellion and the conscious choice to create meaning, individuals can transcend the absurd and find a sense of purpose and fulfilment.

Existentialism plays a vital role in Camus's exploration of the human condition. He rejects the notion that life is predetermined or has an inherent purpose. Instead, he emphasises the importance of personal autonomy and individual responsibility in shaping one's existence. For Camus, the absurd demands that individuals take ownership of their lives and actively engage with the world, even in the face of adversity or suffering.

Camus believes that the human capacity for freedom is both liberating and burdensome. While freedom allows individuals to choose their values and create meaning, it also exposes them to the weight of responsibility. This burden is particularly evident in the face of existential crises, where choices become increasingly significant. Camus argues that individuals must bear this responsibility bravely, recognising that their decisions shape their lives and impact the broader society.

Central to Camus's philosophy is the concept of the absurd hero. The absurd hero is an individual who recognises and confronts the absurdity of existence with courage, defiance, and integrity. This hero does not shy away from life's inherent contradictions and uncertainties but confronts them head-on. In doing so, the hero embodies a form of existential rebellion, challenging prevailing norms and actively seeking to create meaning and value in a seemingly meaningless world.

Camus's exploration of morality and justice further contributes to his unique philosophical framework. Criticising the idea of an absolute, universal morality, Camus instead proposes a more relativistic view. He asserts that moral judgements should be based on empathy, compassion, and a deep understanding of the inherent dignity of every individual. Rejecting rigid dogmas, Camus emphasises the importance of human solidarity and interconnectedness, suggesting that individuals can foster a more just and humane society through compassion and understanding.

Furthermore, Camus's philosophy resonates with a humanistic perspective that emphasises the significance of human connection and compassion. He recognises the struggles and conflicts inherent in life but encourages individuals to embrace their shared humanity and support one another. By acknowledging our interdependence and inherent connection to others, we can find solace and camaraderie and create meaning even amidst the seeming absurdity and chaos of the world.

However, Camus's philosophy should not be misconstrued as promoting nihilism or apathy. Instead, he advocates for an active engagement with the world, encouraging individuals to reject despair and embrace the responsibility to create meaning. Recognising the absurdity of existence is not a call for resignation but a call to action to courageously face life's challenges and strive towards a more meaningful existence.

Interestingly, Camus's philosophy is not confined solely to the realm of academia and abstract thought. It has practical implications for our everyday lives. By acknowledging the absurd and accepting the freedom that comes with it, individuals can liberate themselves from the constraints of societal expectations and live a life true to themselves. This call to authenticity and personal integrity is a recurring theme in Camus's works.

Camus's philosophy also offers us a new lens through which to view tragedy and suffering. Rather than viewing them as inherently negative or unjust, Camus invites us to see them as part of the human experience, inseparable from life's beauty and joy. He encourages us to find meaning in our struggles, transform adversity into resilience, and embrace life's absurdity as an opportunity for growth and self-discovery.

In conclusion, Albert Camus's philosophy and worldview provide an intellectual and emotional journey into the depths of human existence. His exploration of absurdism, existentialism, and humanism invites us to question, reflect, and redefine our understanding of ourselves and our world. By embracing freedom, acknowledging our shared humanity, and rebelling against the absurd, we become actively engaged in creating meaning, purpose, and a more compassionate world. Camus's philosophy challenges us to confront both the existential crises and the ethical dilemmas of our time, urging us to live authentically and make conscious choices that reflect our deepest values. In doing so, we can navigate the complexities of existence with courage, integrity, and a commitment to creating a more just and meaningful world.

SEVENTEEN

EXPLORATION OF ABSURDISM AND THE HUMAN CONDITION

Absurdism, a philosophical concept that challenges traditional notions of meaning and purpose captivated Camus and led him to unravel the complexities of existence. His writings offer a profound examination of this existential dilemma, urging us to confront the absurdity of life and seek authenticity amidst the chaos.

Camus's concept of the absurd arose from his critique of nihilism and existentialism, two philosophical systems that presented differing perspectives on the meaning of human existence. While nihilism insists that life is utterly devoid of value, existentialism advocates for creating meaning through individual processes of choice and self-creation. However, Camus found shortcomings in both approaches and offered an alternative understanding of the absurd – one that embraced the paradoxical nature of our existence.

According to Camus, the human condition is characterised by an inherent tension between our longing for meaning and the world's absurdity. He believed that individuals are perpetually caught in the oscillation between despair, resulting from the inability to find inherent purpose, and the pursuit of happiness and fulfilment, often through the creation of personal meanings. This constant struggle defines our engagement with life, much like the mythical figure of Sisyphus.

In his philosophically influential essay, "The Myth of Sisyphus," Camus portrays human experience as an eternal recurrence of futile tasks like Sisyphus relentlessly pushing a boulder up a hill only to witness its inevitable descent. Through this powerful analogy, Camus compels us to confront the apparent meaninglessness of existence and grapple with the absurd.

However, Camus does not advocate succumbing to despair or seeking illusory distractions. Instead, he exhorts individuals to confront the absurd and strive for authenticity and resilience. In the face of life's inherent meaninglessness, Camus urges us to embrace our freedom, assert our humanity, and find purpose in an act of rebellion against the absurdity of existence.

This notion of rebellion is vital to Camus's philosophy. He contends that even in a world stripped of intrinsic meaning, individuals possess the power to create their own values and mould their lives through acts of defiance and revolt. By rebelling against the absurd, individuals assert their freedom, reaffirm their inherent humanity, and discover a profound fulfilment that transcends the meaninglessness of existence itself.

Camus's profound exploration of absurdism and the human condition has left an indelible mark on existential philosophy and literature. His works continue to resonate with readers, inviting them to confront the bewildering questions of existence and find profound meaning and authenticity within the absurdity of life. By grappling with the inherent paradoxes and contradictions of the human condition, Camus's writings impel us to embrace our freedom, nurture our rebellious spirit, and ultimately discover a way to live fully and authentically in the face of the absurd.

EIGHTEEN

CAMUS'S THOUGHTS ON EXISTENTIALISM, FREEDOM, AND REBELLION

Camus's profound thoughts on existentialism, freedom, and rebellion permeate his extensive work, delving into the complexities of the human condition and offering a deeply nuanced understanding of the struggle for meaning in an inherently absurd world. Through an unwavering commitment to philosophical exploration, Camus's writings reverberate with intellectual depth and existential insights, inviting readers to embark on a profound journey of introspection and contemplation.

At the core of Camus's philosophy, existentialism illuminates the individual's responsibility for constructing meaning in a universe devoid of inherent purpose or rationality. Embracing this philosophy with a blend of earnestness and scepticism, Camus confronts the inherent absurdity of life. He argues that the human quest for meaning is ultimately fruitless, as life's absurdity exposes the fundamental dissonance between our desire for significance and the inherent emptiness of existence.

Yet, within this absurdity, Camus identifies a fragile yet potent concept: the empowering freedom to choose and create personal meaning. He perceives freedom as an essential aspect of human existence—an undeniable quality that distinguishes us. However, Camus warns against an illusion of absolute freedom, recognising the constraints imposed by external circumstances. While individuals possess agency to make choices, they are also shaped by their particular contexts, historical circumstances, and social structures that limit the range of possibilities available to them.

Camus challenges the prevalent notion of unfettered freedom and emphasises the need for individuals to grapple with and embrace the boundaries set before them. By acknowledging the constraints, individuals can engage in an existential negotiation between personal agency and external forces, paving the way for a more nuanced understanding of freedom within the intricate tapestry of existence.

Rebellion emerges as a recurrent motif in Camus's philosophical landscape. Through rebellion, individuals confront the absurdity and injustices of the world, forging an authentic response to the collision between human desires and the chaos surrounding us. However, for

Camus, rebellion extends beyond mere political or social activism—it embodies a profound philosophical and existential act. By rebelling, individuals assert their freedom and affirm their existence amidst life's absurdities.

Camus sees rebellion as an intrinsic human response, a means of transcending the inherent absurdity of existence and challenging oppressive systems. It is a courageous act that allows individuals to construct their own moral values, shape their sense of purpose, and forge a meaningful life in the face of an ultimately indifferent universe. Through rebellion, individuals embrace the paradoxical nature of their existence, weaving together personal agency and the larger context within which they operate.

Camus's philosophical ideas on existentialism, freedom, and rebellion come to life in his renowned works. In "The Stranger," the character of Meursault embodies the sense of existential absurdity, defying social conventions through his rebellion. Additionally, in "The Myth of Sisyphus," Camus delves deeper into the concept of rebellion as a mechanism to confront absurdity head-on, ultimately advocating for embracing life's intrinsic contradictions.

Camus's exploration of existentialism, freedom, and rebellion resonates deeply with readers and stimulates profound introspection. His ideas invite us to grapple with the intricacies of existence, navigate the delicate balance between personal freedom and external constraints, and reflect upon the transformative potential of rebellion in shaping our individual and collective lives. Through his penetrating insights, Camus invites us to embark on a profound journey of introspection and contemplation, unravelling the mysteries that lie at the heart of our human experience.

NINETEEN

THE CONCEPT OF THE ABSURD HERO IN CAMUS'S PHILOSOPHY

As elucidated by Albert Camus, the concept of the absurd hero delves into profound questions surrounding the nature of existence and the search for meaning in an indifferent universe. In his seminal essay, "The Myth of Sisyphus," Camus explores the idea of the absurd, which arises from the fundamental disparity between humanity's longing for purpose and the universe's impartiality towards our existence. This juxtaposition gives birth to an internal struggle within individuals, ultimately leading to the formation of the absurd hero.

At the core of Camus's philosophy lies the recognition of a void, an inherent emptiness in the fabric of existence. To confront this existential void head-on is an overwhelming task; it is to venture into the realm of the absurd, where life appears devoid of ultimate purpose. In the face of such absurdity, the absurd hero emerges—chosen not by fate or external circumstances but by a deliberate decision to confront and rebel against the meaninglessness.

The absurd hero is not a conventional protagonist embarking on heroic quests or external battles. Rather, their heroism lies in an introspective journey of self-discovery, navigating the intricacies of human existence. This hero acknowledges the absurdity of life but refuses to succumb to it. This hero strives to carve out a meaningful existence amidst the void through rebellion.

Authenticity serves as the guiding light for the absurd hero. By embracing one's true self and living authentically, individuals can confront life's absurdity and find moments of transcendence. Authenticity necessitates a profound engagement with the present moment as the hero shifts their focus towards tangible experiences and realities. Through this lived experience, the absurd hero unearths the elusive value of existence, binding meaning to the seemingly insignificant facets of life.

One exemplary manifestation of the absurd hero can be found in Camus's novel, "The Stranger," embodied by its protagonist, Meursault. Meursault's apathy towards societal expectations and norms functions as an act of rebellion against the meaninglessness of existence. He resolutely rejects conformity and recognises the absurdity prevailing within society. Meursault's consciousness of life's lack of ultimate purpose fuels his defiance against the imposed expectations of others.

Within Meursault's journey, Camus highlights instances where meaning and fulfilment are discovered in simplicity. Stripped of grandiose connotations, Meursault revels in sensory experiences—basking in the warmth of sunlight on his face, listening to the enchanting cadence of crashing waves, savouring the taste of a cup of coffee. These intimately cherished moments hold intrinsic value for the absurd hero, representing a rebellion against the void and affirming existence's fleeting, visceral beauty.

The idea of the absurd hero challenges conventional notions of heroism, which are often characterised by achievements, triumphs, and victories. Instead, Camus unveils the true essence of heroism as an inner struggle to unearth meaning and authenticity within a fundamentally meaningless world. The absurd hero's rebellion against existence's absurdity resonates as a resounding act of courage, surpassing societal expectations and embracing a personal truth—a truth that is unique and profound.

Camus's concept of the absurd hero has profoundly impacted existential philosophy and literature, stretching the boundaries of our understanding. It encourages individuals to confront and accept the inherent absurdity at the heart of existence while simultaneously finding purpose and value in their lives. Through the absurd hero, Camus showcases the resilience and defiance of the human spirit in the face of an indifferent universe, serving as a testament to the human capacity for freedom, rebellion, and courage. As we engage with the absurd hero, Camus beckons us to probe our own lives, challenging us to live more authentically, bravely embracing the absurdity intertwined with the human experience.

Twenty

Camus's Views on Morality and Justice

Albert Camus explored complex ideas surrounding morality and justice with profound insight and nuance in his philosophical and literary works. Central to Camus's thought was the concept of the absurd—an understanding that life is inherently devoid of any ultimate meaning or purpose. This perspective influenced his views on morality and how individuals should navigate the world facing such existential challenges.

Camus rejected the idea of any fixed moral system or religious doctrine, recognising their limitations in providing satisfactory answers to the deeper questions of human existence. Rather than relying on external moral guidelines, he emphasised personal responsibility and the need for individuals to create their own ethical frameworks. This involved drawing upon their lived experiences, rigorous observations, and reflective thinking to form their moral compass.

For Camus, the absence of an objective moral order meant that individuals had to confront the inherent absurdity of existence and make choices without relying on external moral guidelines. While some might see this as a cause for despair or nihilism, Camus saw it as an opportunity for profound freedom and authenticity. He believed that individuals should embrace the belief that they are solely responsible for their actions and decisions.

Despite the lack of inherent meaning, Camus placed great importance on recognising the value and dignity of every human life. He believed that this recognition formed the foundation of any meaningful ethical development. By acknowledging the shared struggles and vulnerabilities inherent in the human condition, individuals could find purpose and meaning as they navigated the world's complexities.

This ethic of human solidarity and empathy formed the bedrock of Camus's approach to morality. He argued that genuine morality necessitated individuals to extend their compassion beyond themselves and their immediate communities. This involved recognising all human beings' universal struggles and vulnerabilities and acting to promote their well-being and dignity. In this sense, for Camus, morality was not some abstract set of rules or principles, but a deeply personal and social endeavor—an ongoing, active practise that required individuals to transcend their own self-interests and contribute to the betterment of others.

Camus also contemplated the nature of justice in a world that seemed devoid of inherent meaning. He acknowledged that pursuing justice could be exceptionally challenging in an absurd and chaotic universe, where the outcomes of our actions often appear arbitrary and unjust. Nevertheless, he argued that the quest for justice was crucial to human dignity and creating a more just society.

However, Camus was wary of dogmatic ideologies and radical methods of pursuing justice. He unequivocally rejected violence and extremism, underscoring the importance of maintaining a moral compass even in the face of oppressive forces. For Camus, true justice must be rooted in compassion, understanding, and an unwavering commitment to human rights. It required a genuine willingness to engage in dialogue, seek common ground, and bridge the divides perpetuating injustice.

Moreover, Camus criticised the concept of absolute justice, which he believed could lead to the dehumanisation of individuals and the use of violence in its name. Instead, he advocated for a more nuanced understanding of justice that prioritised empathy, compassion, and a profound respect for the inherent worth of every individual. This meant recognising that justice is complex and multifaceted, requiring a fair consideration of individuals' circumstances, context, and diverse needs.

In his literary works, such as "The Plague" and "The Fall," Camus skillfully portrayed characters grappling with their moral responsibilities and the consequences of their actions. Through their narratives, he highlighted the ambiguities and contradictions inherent in ethical decision-making, forcing readers to confront their ethical beliefs and assumptions.

Camus's views on morality and justice continue to provoke philosophical debate and inspire readers to examine the foundations of their own ethical frameworks. His emphasis on personal responsibility, the recognition of human dignity, and the pursuit of justice offers a unique and profound perspective on moral philosophy. Camus challenges individuals to confront the absurdity of existence, embrace their freedom and agency, and endeavour to create a more humane and just world through their choices and actions. Furthermore, his writings invite us to question the limitations of rigid moral systems and religious doctrines and instead encourage us to actively engage in ethical reflection and cultivate a moral compass that values our shared humanity.

Twenty-One

Style and Influence: A Literary Giant and Existential Thought Leader

Albert Camus, whose powerful literary works continue to captivate readers worldwide, stands as one of the most influential and accomplished writers of the 20th century. His unique and compelling writing style and profound philosophical ideas have left an indelible mark on modern literature, shaping the existentialist movement and challenging readers to confront the complexities of the human condition.

Camus's literary style goes beyond its simplicity, clarity, and accessibility, as these qualities merely scratch the surface of his artistry. While he was committed to expressing his ideas in a language that could be understood and felt by a wide audience, his choice of words carried a depth and complexity that rewarded thoughtful engagement. Through carefully crafted sentences and precise diction, Camus wove together a tapestry of meaning that invites readers to ponder the fundamental questions of existence.

Moreover, Camus's writing style was characterised by an intense focus on the precision of language. He believed that every word mattered, every sentence carried weight, and every paragraph contributed to the work's overall impact. His dedication to linguistic precision allowed him to convey his ideas with clarity and resonance, avoiding the pitfalls of ambiguity or vagueness. This meticulous attention to detail enhanced the impact of his prose, creating a profound and lasting impression on the reader's mind.

In addition to his linguistic prowess, Camus skillfully employed various narrative techniques to convey his themes and ideas. One notable technique was his use of irony and juxtaposition, which added depth and complexity to his writings. By presenting contrasting situations or ideas side by side, Camus revealed the dissonance inherent in the human experience. These ironic elements allowed readers to confront the paradoxes and contradictions of life, challenging them to seek meaning within the absurdity.

Another distinctive aspect of Camus's writing style was his ability to evoke vivid imagery and sensory descriptions. He possessed a keen eye for detail and a deep appreciation for the natural world, which he skillfully incorporated into his works. Through his precise observations of nature, Camus not only enhanced the atmosphere and mood of his stories but also used these descriptions as metaphors for the human condition. The natural world became a mirror reflecting his characters' inner turmoil and existential dilemmas, forging a powerful connection between the external and internal realms.

Beyond its literary merits, Camus's impact extended far into the realms of philosophy and existential thought. His works challenged traditional narratives and ideologies, inviting readers to question the meaning and purpose of their existence. Central to Camus's philosophy was the concept of the absurd, the recognition that life lacks inherent meaning and purpose, and the subsequent invitation to create our own significance in an indifferent universe. Through his writings, he confronted the existential anxieties and moral dilemmas that arise from this realisation, offering insights and perspectives that have continued to resonate with readers throughout the decades.

Furthermore, Camus's influence on contemporary literature cannot be overstated. His groundbreaking works inspired countless writers to explore similar existential themes and adopt a more accessible writing style. His ideas found expression not only in literature but also in other artistic mediums. Filmmakers, playwrights, and musicians drew inspiration from his writings, infusing their creations with existential ideas and creating an interwoven tapestry of existential thought in various art forms.

As we reflect upon Camus's enduring legacy, it becomes evident that his contributions to literature and philosophy are intertwined and inseparable. His distinct writing style, crafted with precision and clarity, continues to captivate and challenge readers. His profound insights into the human condition, the absurd, and the quest for meaning resonate across time and remain relevant in our contemporary world. Camus was more than just a writer; he was a philosopher, an existentialist thought leader, and a powerful voice that encourages us to confront the complexities of our existence.

In conclusion, Albert Camus's literary style and influence were characterised by his commitment to simplicity, clarity, and immersive storytelling techniques. Yet, beyond these surface qualities, his writing possessed a depth and complexity that rewarded careful consideration. Through linguistic precision, narrative techniques, evocative imagery, and a profound exploration of existential themes, Camus continues to shape our understanding of the human condition and inspire readers to ponder the meaning of their own existence. His enduring legacy as a literary giant and existential thought leader challenges us to confront the absurdity of life with courage and create our own meaningful narratives amidst an indifferent universe.

Twenty-Two

Analysis of Camus's Narrative Techniques and Stylistic Choices

Albert Camus, the acclaimed philosopher and writer, was known for his exceptional narrative techniques and stylistic choices that enhanced his writings' rich themes of existentialism and absurdity.

A notable aspect of Camus's narrative style is his masterful use of sparse and concise language, a powerful tool for conveying his philosophical ideas. Every word he employs is deliberate and purposeful, carrying significant weight and imbuing his prose with a haunting poetic quality. Through short, precise sentences, Camus achieves a sense of urgency, effectively capturing the existential dilemmas and the bleakness of the human condition that pervades his narratives. This minimalist approach allows his writing to distil complex philosophical concepts into their elemental essence, resonating directly with the intellect and emotions of his readers.

Additionally, Camus's writing is marked by evocative and vivid imagery that vividly brings his narratives to life. Whether describing the oppressive Algerian sun relentlessly scorching the city streets or the suffocating atmosphere that permeates a town during a plague outbreak, his descriptive language immerses the reader in his narratives' physical and emotional landscapes. This skilful portrayal of sensory details not only creates a strong sense of place but also emphasises the absurdity and existential angst experienced by his characters. The images themselves become symbolic, representing the harsh realities of existence and deepening the philosophical undertones of his works.

Moreover, Camus's narrative technique often embraces a detached and objective perspective that gives readers an outsider's view of the events unfolding. Camus encourages introspection and critical examination of the human experience through a narrative voice that remains aloof and distant. This calculated distance not only highlights the theme of absurdity but also allows readers to confront their own mortality and the futility of life's pursuits, amplifying the impact of Camus's writing. By holding readers at a certain remove, he enables them to reflect upon their own existence and grapple with the essential questions of humanity.

In addition to his sparse language and detached perspective, Camus frequently employs a nonlinear narrative structure, challenging conventional ideas of chronology. By juxtaposing events out of sequence, he prompts readers to consider the fluidity of time and how memory shapes our understanding of existence. This nonlinearity reinforces the notion that life itself is inherently fragmented, highlighting the disorientation and meaninglessness that lie at the heart of Camus's philosophy of the absurd. As readers navigate through the labyrinthine structure of his narratives, they are compelled to confront the essential questions of purpose and meaning in life.

Furthermore, Camus masterfully utilises symbolism and allegory as vehicles to explore deeper existential meanings within his writings. The symbols he employs resonate with readers, transcending their literal meanings to represent profound and abstract concepts. In "The Stranger," the sun symbolises the indifferent universe, casting its relentless glare on the protagonist's isolation and alienation. Likewise, the plague in "The Plague" becomes a metaphor for the existential struggles of humanity under the weight of suffering and death. These symbols add layers of depth and complexity to Camus's narratives, guiding readers through the labyrinthine landscape of his philosophy and allowing for multiple interpretations and contemplation.

Beyond symbolism, Camus seamlessly blends elements of realism and existentialism within his writing. He intertwines philosophical ideas with everyday experiences and interactions, grounding his concepts in relatable situations. This fusion results in a unique and thought-provoking blend of existentialism and realistic storytelling, presenting the universal human condition in a tangible and accessible manner. The familiar settings and relatable characters draw readers into his narratives and create a space where existential crises and the absurdity of life can be confronted and explored.

In conclusion, the narrative techniques and stylistic choices employed by Albert Camus contribute significantly to the profound impact and enduring influence of his works. From his sparse and concise language to evocative imagery, detached perspective, nonlinear structure, symbolism, and the fusion of realism and existentialism, each element enhances the depth and complexity of his narratives. Camus's ability to merge philosophy and storytelling immerses readers in the enigmatic realm of existential thought, leaving an indelible mark on literary history and continuing to inspire introspection and contemplation of the human condition.

TWENTY-THREE

CAMUS'S INFLUENCE ON MODERN LITERATURE AND EXISTENTIAL THOUGHT

Albert Camus, one of the most influential writers of the 20th century, has left an indelible mark on modern literature and existential thought. His exploration of the human condition and his concept of absurdism have deeply resonated with countless writers and thinkers, shaping the landscape of literature and philosophy.

Camus's impact on literature is evident in the works of authors who have drawn inspiration from his philosophy and narrative style. A renowned existentialist, Jean-Paul Sartre, engaged in a philosophical dialogue with Camus, further developing existentialism in literature. Through exchanges of ideas and divergent approaches, Sartre and Camus contributed to a broader understanding of existential thought, sparking discussions on freedom, responsibility, and the meaning of existence.

The concept of the absurd, vividly portrayed in Camus's seminal work "The Stranger," continues to resonate in modern literature. This notion, which suggests that the human search for meaning may ultimately be fruitless, has found echoes in the works of contemporary authors such as Haruki Murakami and Kazuo Ishiguro. These writers explore themes of isolation, alienation, and the inexplicability of life, taking inspiration from Camus to explore the complex dynamics of human existence.

Camus's influence on literature extends beyond existential themes. His writing style, characterised by concise and evocative prose, has inspired many authors. The economy of his language, combined with his ability to convey complex ideas with simplicity, has influenced contemporary writers seeking to engage readers on a deeper level. Authors like J.M. Coetzee and Margaret Atwood have emulated Camus's use of ambiguity, irony, and symbolism, which allow them to navigate existential questions and highlight the human condition within their own narratives.

Moreover, Camus's impact can be observed within the realm of theatre, specifically through the rise of absurd theatre. Playwrights such as Eugène Ionesco, Samuel Beckett, and Harold Pinter have incorporated elements of the absurd into their works. Inspired by Camus's exploration of the cognitive dissonance arising from the clash between human desire for meaning and a seemingly indifferent universe, absurd theatre challenges conventional dramatic norms. It explores the inexplicable and illogical aspects of human existence.

Existential thought, emphasising individual freedom and responsibility, owes much to Camus. His ideas of rebellion and the absurd hero have resonated with philosophers and thinkers seeking to delve into similar themes. Influential figures like Simone de Beauvoir, Maurice Merleau-Ponty, and Jean-Paul Sartre have drawn upon Camus's views on existentialism and the human condition, building upon his ideas to shape their own philosophical frameworks. It is through this intellectual dialogue that existential thought has evolved and adapted over time.

Beyond literature, Camus's ideas have permeated broader cultural realms. His emphasis on personal authenticity and the pursuit of meaning in an absurd world has touched the lives of individuals grappling with existential questions. Camus's philosophy continues to be studied and debated in philosophical and academic circles, influencing ongoing discussions on the nature of human existence and the quest for happiness. Moreover, his influence extends to psychology, sociology, and even political thought, where his ideas on rebellion and the role of the individual have fostered critical perspectives on societal structures and power dynamics.

Camus's literary style and narrative techniques have also left an enduring impact on modern literature. His concise and evocative prose and his ability to simplify complex ideas have influenced generations of writers. Camus's use of ambiguity, irony, and symbolism, particularly evident in works such as "The Plague" and "The Fall," has been emulated by writers exploring existential themes in their own works. His storytelling techniques have continued to inspire authors who seek to engage readers on a deeper level, challenging them to ponder the fundamental questions of human existence.

In conclusion, Albert Camus's influence on modern literature and existential thought is profound and far-reaching. His exploration of the absurd, his philosophical reflections, and his distinctive literary style have shaped the work of countless writers and thinkers. Camus's enduring legacy continues to inspire and challenge contemporary literature and philosophical discourse, cementing him as a pivotal figure in the cultural landscape of the modern era.

TWENTY-FOUR

COMPARISON WITH CONTEMPORARY PHILOSOPHERS AND WRITERS

In examining the profound influence and far-reaching impact of Albert Camus, it becomes crucial to delve even deeper into his exceptional contributions and how his philosophy and literature intersect with the work of his fellow contemporary thinkers. Examining Camus's unique ideas and thought-provoking themes invites us to explore the myriad connections and resonances he shares with philosophers and writers within and outside the existentialist tradition.

One prominent philosopher who shares common ground with Camus is Jean-Paul Sartre. Although Sartre and Camus ultimately had a falling out, primarily due to their divergent political beliefs, their initial alignment as leading figures of the existentialist movement cannot be overlooked. Both Sartre and Camus probed the depths of existential questions and explored the theme of absurdity in the human condition. Their philosophical investigations into the meaning and purpose of life, the concept of freedom within a seemingly meaningless universe, and the struggles individuals face in finding meaning resonated deeply with each other's work. Indeed, the fundamental questions of existence, freedom, and the pursuit of meaning formed the core of their shared concerns.

Sartre's concept of existentialism as a commitment to personal freedom and responsibility echoes the foundational tenets of Camus's philosophy. Emphasising that existence precedes essence, Sartre insisted on the individual's responsibility to shape their own meaning in a world stripped of inherent purpose. Similarly, Camus's exploration of the absurd highlighted the human predicament of seeking meaning and purpose in an indifferent and seemingly nonsensical universe. While Sartre exalted the pursuit of individual freedom through political activism and embraced Marxism, Camus remained sceptical of revolutionary ideologies and turned his focus toward searching for personal meaning by actively rebelling against the absurd. Despite their differences, both Sartre and Camus made invaluable contributions to existentialism, challenging individuals to confront the complexities of existence and encouraging them to question societal norms.

Friedrich Nietzsche is another influential thinker who engaged with Camus's ideas, although predating him by several decades. Nietzsche's concepts of the eternal return, the death of God, and the search for meaning reverberate strongly within Camus's works. Both philosophers confront nihilism and the absurdity of existence head-on. While Camus rejected the nihilistic implications of the absurd, asserting the importance of revolt against the meaninglessness of life, Nietzsche tackled nihilism by proposing the idea of eternal recurrence as a means to overcome its destructive consequences. Camus's rejection of nihilism is evident in his emphasis on rebellion and pursuing personal and collective meaning in a fundamentally meaningless world. Nietzsche's influence can be discerned in Camus's exploration of the individual's power to shape their own fate and the rejection of passive acceptance.

In the realm of literature, the impact of Camus's themes and narrative style can be seen reflected in the works of numerous contemporary authors. One such writer who shares common ground with Camus is Haruki Murakami, celebrated for blending realism and surrealism and exploring existential themes. Murakami's characters often grapple with a sense of alienation, isolation, and the relentless search for authenticity, evoking the spirit of Camus's protagonists. Both authors delve into the depths of the human condition, unearthing its inherent contradictions and posing profound questions about the nature of existence.

Likewise, the thought-provoking works of American novelist and essayist David Foster Wallace reveal striking parallels to Camus's ideas. Wallace's exploration of human suffering, the nature of consciousness, and the tensions between individual freedom and societal constraints mirrors Camus's concerns. Both authors adeptly challenge conventional thinking, offering nuanced perspectives on contemporary life and the intricate challenges of being human. Wallace's emphasis on the complexities of human experience and the search for meaning resonates deeply with Camus's philosophy, which advocates for embracing the struggle against the absurd and finding meaning even in the face of overwhelming uncertainty.

It is vital to acknowledge that Camus's profound impact extends beyond the realms of philosophy and literature. His works have captivated filmmakers, musicians, and visual artists, who have found inspiration in his exploration of the absurd and the human condition. Films like "The Matrix," delving into the nature of reality and the quest for freedom, bear traces of Camus's influence. Similarly, musicians like Nick Cave, whose lyrics evoke existential questions and themes, effectively draw from the legacy of Camus, highlighting the enduring relevance of his ideas. The creative reception and interpretation across various artistic mediums demonstrate the profound and enduring nature of Camus's intellectual and artistic contributions.

In comparing Camus's philosophy and literature with the ideas and works of contemporary philosophers and writers, we gain a deeper appreciation for his unique imprint on the intellectual and artistic landscapes. While differences in emphasis and perspective exist among these thinkers, their shared exploration of existential questions and the struggle to find meaning and purpose in a seemingly absurd world solidify Camus's position as a figure of enduring relevance in contemporary thought and creative expression.

Twenty-Five

Camus's Political Engagements and Controversies

Albert Camus was not merely an observer of the world but an actively engaged political figure. Throughout his life, he immersed himself in debates and stood firmly on various social issues. However, his political engagements were neither simple nor without controversy. Camus often found himself entangled amidst conflicting ideologies, which led to criticism from different sides of the political spectrum.

One of the most significant controversies surrounding Camus was his stance on colonialism and the Algerian War, a subject deeply intertwined with his own personal history. Born on November 7, 1913, in Mondovi, French Algeria, Camus grew up in a society marked by the intricate dynamics of colonial rule. As a youth, he faced discrimination and witnessed firsthand the oppressive nature of the colonial regime.

Early in his journalistic career, Camus devoted considerable attention to social and political issues relating to Algerian society. Impacted by his own experiences and deeply empathetic to the plight of the Algerian people, Camus initially sympathised with their struggle for independence. In 1939, he joined the Communist Party, primarily drawn to their fight against fascism and their efforts to address social inequality.

However, as time passed, Camus's perspective on the issue evolved. He continued to firmly believe in justice and equality, advocating for a peaceful resolution to the conflict. Camus ardently promoted dialogue between the French government and the Algerian nationalists, hoping for a compromise that would respect the rights and aspirations of both parties involved. Despite his intentions, his stance on the conflict was criticised by various quarters.

The complexity of the Algerian War posed a difficult moral and political challenge for Camus. His nuanced and moderate position often placed him in a precarious middle ground, susceptible to criticism from the French authorities and some Algerian intellectuals. To some, Camus's moderation appeared insufficient, believing he should have taken a more radical stance supporting Algerian independence. On the other hand, some Algerian nationalists considered his position a betrayal of his own heritage, arguing that he failed to align himself with their cause fully.

In navigating the Algerian conflict, Camus faced a conundrum emblematic of his larger political engagements: the struggle to find a middle ground. Despite the heat of criticism, Camus steadfastly pursued his vision of reconciliation, advocating for a resolution that upheld the principles of justice and acknowledged the rights of all parties involved. Nonetheless, these efforts left him isolated and caught between rival factions, often lacking full support.

Camus's political engagements extended beyond the Algerian War and into the post-World War II era. In the aftermath of the war, he became involved in socialist and communist circles, sharing empathy for their aspirations for social justice. However, his association with these groups was not without tension. While he aligned himself ideologically with their goals, he vehemently criticised the oppressive tactics employed by certain communist regimes.

His famous essay, "The Rebel," published in 1951, explored the dangers of revolutionary violence and its potential to lead to totalitarianism. Camus argued that any movement aiming to achieve freedom and justice must remain rooted in respect for human dignity and individual freedoms. This critical stance on totalitarianism created a rift between him and prominent leftist intellectuals of his time, most notably Jean-Paul Sartre, who championed Marxist ideologies and saw violence as a necessary means to an end.

Refusing to submit to ideological dogma, Camus maintained an independent and critical perspective, driven by a deep concern for human dignity and the preservation of principles he held dear. He sought a balance between the ideals of individualism and the pursuit of social justice, viewing them as intimately linked rather than mutually exclusive. This nuanced stance garnered him immense respect from some quarters while generating criticism from others.

The controversies surrounding Camus's political engagements attest to the complexity and multifaceted nature of his approach to social issues. His stance on colonialism and the Algerian conflict, as well as his critique of totalitarianism, underlines his steadfast dedication to the values of justice, equality, and individual freedom. Camus's political engagements were founded on a genuine search for common ground and pursuing a just and equitable society despite the resulting criticisms and misunderstandings.

In the annals of political history, Camus's actions testify to the depth and complexity of his intellectual and political legacy. His unwavering commitment to his principles, even at the cost of alienation, puts his political engagements in a league of their own. Albert Camus inspires introspection and critical thinking through his writings and actions, challenging individuals to navigate the complexities of political engagement and seek justice and compassion in a world fraught with discord and division.

TWENTY-SIX

CAMUS'S STANCE ON COLONIALISM AND THE ALGERIAN WAR

Albert Camus had a complex and diverse view on colonialism and the Algerian War. This topic strongly impacted both his personal life and literary works. Being born in Algeria, Camus possessed a distinctive outlook on the matter of colonialism. He personally witnessed the benefits and injustices that came with French rule. Through his exploration of this subject, he highlighted the conflicting aspects and difficult decisions one encounters when grappling with questions of identity, loyalty, and justice.

In the early stages of his career, Camus sympathised with the cause of Algerian independence and joined the Algerian Communist Party. He wrote articles advocating for the rights of the Algerian people, condemning the oppressive nature of colonial rule and highlighting the social and economic inequalities perpetuated by it. His early stance on colonialism reflected his egalitarian ideals and belief in all individuals' fundamental dignity, regardless of nationality or ethnicity.

However, as the conflict escalated and became more violent, Camus was torn between his Algerian heritage and his strong affiliation with French culture. Being a prominent French intellectual, he faced mounting pressure from both sides of the conflict. Algerian nationalists and anti-colonialists expected him to fully align himself with their cause and actively join the struggle for independence, while some French intellectuals accused him of disloyalty to France by advocating for Algerian rights.

Camus's internal struggle was further complicated by his existential philosophy and belief in the human condition's inherent absurdity. He acknowledged that violence and oppression were central features of the human experience, but he refused to accept them as inevitable or justifiable. In this light, the Algerian War presented a painful paradox for Camus: he recognised the Algerian people's just demand for self-determination. He resented French colonialism, yet he also deplored the bloodshed and suffering that resulted from the conflict.

Given his commitment to humanism, Camus sought a path that would reconcile these conflicting loyalties and provide a framework for a peaceful resolution. He argued for a dialogue between the French and Algerians, urging both sides to recognise their shared humanity and work towards a just and equitable solution. Camus acknowledged the grievances and injustices suffered by the Algerian people and emphasised the urgent need for reconciliation, rejecting the notion that violence could bring about a lasting solution.

Although rooted in his espousal of peace and justice, Camus's stance on the Algerian War encountered criticism from various quarters. Algerian nationalists accused him of not fully committing to their cause, believing that his position was intellectual detachment rather than active support. Meanwhile, some French intellectuals accused him of undermining the French state and labelled him disloyal for standing up for Algerian rights.

However, it is essential to delve deeper into the psychological and emotional impact the Algerian War had on Camus personally. The conflict brought about a profound existential crisis for him, deepening his understanding of human nature's inherent contradictions and complexities. He grappled with questions of identity and belonging, torn between his Algerian roots and French education and culture. In his essay, "Letters to a German Friend," Camus opens up about this internal struggle, stating, "In my homeland, I am scorned for my Frenchness, and in France condemned as an outsider. But I belong to both and am at home nowhere."

Camus's notion of the Absurd, central to his philosophy, further shaped his perspective on the Algerian War. The conflict magnified the inherent absurdity of human existence, as both the French and Algerian sides engaged in violence and suffering. Camus believed that acknowledging the Absurd meant recognising the limitations of our rationality, the contingency of our existence, and the ambiguity of moral values. In the face of this Absurd, he sought to promote empathy, dialogue, and solidarity as possible avenues for transcending the boundaries of conflict and achieving a more just and compassionate society.

The Algerian War pushed Camus to confront his own humanity and grapple with the dilemmas of justice and responsibility. He believed that violence only perpetuated further violence, emphasising that the true measure of civilisation lies not in military conquest but in our capacity to engage in dialogue, understanding, and reconciliation. Camus's rejection of violence to achieve freedom and justice was informed by his conviction that it ultimately dehumanises the oppressor and oppressed.

It is important to note that despite the complexity and internal turmoil Camus experienced during the war, his commitment to justice and equality never wavered. He firmly believed in the fundamental rights and dignity of all individuals, regardless of nationality or ethnicity, and remained dedicated to advocating for a peaceful and humane resolution to the conflict. In his Nobel Prize acceptance speech, Camus reflected on the values that guided his stance, stating, "Today I believe in the possibility of love; that is why I fervently defend the cause of those who suffer these absurd injustices."

In conclusion, Albert Camus's stance on colonialism and the Algerian War was deeply rooted in his personal experiences, philosophical convictions, and commitment to justice and solidarity. His exploration of these complex issues highlights the intricate balance between conflicting loyalties and the challenges of promoting peaceful resolutions in the face of violence and injustice. Camus's writings and actions serve as a reminder of the importance of empathy, dialogue, and the pursuit of a more just and compassionate world.

Twenty-Seven

Engagement with Political and Social Issues of His Time

Camus stood as a prominent figure for his literary contributions and his unwavering commitment to engaging with his time's pressing political and social issues. Throughout his life, he tirelessly used his platform to advocate for social justice, equality, and individual rights.

Because of his birth in French Algeria, Camus endured a difficult childhood marked by poverty and the cultural tensions between the French colonial ruling class and the Algerian population. His experiences in Algeria, a colony caught between conflicting identities and aspirations, would profoundly shape his understanding of oppression, injustice, and the complexities of resistance.

From an early age, Camus showed a profound empathy for the plight of the marginalised. His position as a journalist allowed him to witness firsthand the devastating consequences of poverty and social inequality. His early works, such as "The Stranger" and "The Myth of Sisyphus," explored the existential condition of humans in an indifferent world while subtly critiquing societal structures that perpetuated oppression.

One of Camus's central themes revolved around his resolute opposition to tyranny and oppression in any form. He vehemently denounced totalitarian ideologies such as fascism, communism, and colonialism, which he deemed as grave threats to human dignity and freedom. Growing up in French Algeria exposed Camus to the intricate complexities inherent in the issue of colonialism, shaping his lifelong pursuit of fairness and equitable relationships between colonisers and the colonised.

Camus's critique of colonialism was particularly evident in his novels, notably "The Plague" and "The Rebel." In "The Plague," published in 1947, Camus explored the devastating impact of a fictional plague sweeping through the Algerian city of Oran. The novel serves as a powerful allegory for the oppressive nature of colonial rule, with the plague representing the destructive forces of injustice and the indifference of those in power. Camus used his writing to capture the characters' personal and communal struggles and highlight the urgent need for resistance against oppressive systems.

Camus called for an end to the mistreatment and exploitation of the indigenous Algerian population by the French colonisers. He firmly believed that everyone deserved recognition and respect, regardless of nationality or ethnicity. However, his critique of colonialism sparked controversy in various circles. Some accused him of betraying his Algerian heritage, while others believed he did not go far enough in denouncing the colonial enterprise.

Nevertheless, Camus's engagement with political and social issues extended beyond Algeria. He actively spoke out against injustices prevalent in French society, challenging the government's handling of economic disparities. Recognising the transformative power of education, he emphasised the importance of promoting accessible education for all and advocated for improved social welfare systems to uplift the marginalised and vulnerable.

Camus also voiced his concerns regarding the rise of totalitarianism across Europe. He condemned the brutalities of fascism during World War II, drawing from his own experiences as a member of the French Resistance. In his essay "The Rebel," published in 1951, Camus delved deeply into the themes of rebellion, revolution, and the responsibility of individuals to challenge oppressive systems. He questioned the legitimacy of violent revolution and called for a moral and ethical approach to resistance that sought justice while remaining true to the values of humanity.

During the Algerian War of Independence, Camus faced a moral dilemma. While he empathised with the Algerians' struggle for freedom, he also feared the escalation of violence and the potential rise of extremism that could further destroy any chance of peaceful coexistence.

Thus, he advocated for dialogue and reconciliation, urging both sides to find a path towards a peaceful resolution. Yet, his nuanced position left him vulnerable to criticism from both sides, with some viewing his calls for peace as a betrayal of the Algerian cause.

Beyond his writing, Camus actively participated in political and intellectual circles, engaging in debates and discussions. He collaborated with prominent figures such as Jean-Paul Sartre, Simone de Beauvoir, and Aimé Césaire, fostering an environment of intellectual exchange and challenging each other's perspectives.

Throughout his life, Camus's engagement with political and social issues was not without contradictions and complexities. Despite his strong opposition to oppression, he grappled with the realities of complex sociopolitical conflicts. Consequently, he faced criticism from various quarters, with some labelling his stances as insufficient or contradictory. Nevertheless, at the core of his convictions lay an unwavering belief in the intrinsic worth and dignity of every human being and a deep desire for a just and compassionate society.

In conclusion, Camus's powerful engagement with his time's political and social issues underscored his unwavering commitment to justice, equality, and individual rights. His contributions continue to inspire generations, reminding us of the importance of standing against injustice and working towards a more equitable world. Camus's legacy reminds us that as intellectual beings, it is our privilege and duty to actively engage with our time's political and social struggles, challenge oppressive systems, and advocate for lasting societal change.

Twenty-Eight

Critiques and Controversies Surrounding His Political Views

As a renowned writer and philosopher and an active participant in political debates and controversies, Camus's engagements spanned a wide range of topics, with particular attention given to colonialism, the Algerian War, and the broader context of French politics. As a result of his involvement, Camus's political views both attracted praise for their depth of thought and drew critiques for their perceived inconsistencies and equivocal stance.

One of the main areas of critique directed towards Camus concerns his position on colonialism. Born and raised in French Algeria, he possessed a unique perspective that gave him a firsthand experience of the complexities inherent in colonial rule. However, Camus's views on colonialism were difficult to categorise within a single ideological framework. He sometimes expressed sympathy towards the Algerian people and their struggle for independence. He participated in various anti-colonial activities, passionately denouncing the injustices perpetuated by colonial powers. Yet, he also emphasised the cultural ties between Algeria and France, leading some critics to accuse him of being an apologist for French colonialism.

Camus's nuanced position on colonialism stemmed from his belief in a shared Mediterranean culture and the desire for a more humane and just relationship between Algeria and France. He recognised Algeria's need for independence but advocated for a cooperative and collaborative approach. This stance drew criticism from both sides, with Algerian nationalists viewing Camus as not fully supporting their cause, while French settlers in Algeria condemned him for sympathising with Algerian nationalism.

The complexities of Camus's political views were further underscored during the Algerian War of Independence. Initially advocating for a peaceful solution, he called for dialogue and understanding to resolve the conflict. However, as the war escalated, Camus grappled with the increasing violence and polarisation within society. Some critics chastised him for not taking a definitive side, deeming his position as equivocal and lacking in full support for the Algerian struggle. Others, however, appreciated his efforts to find a path of reconciliation amidst the deep divisions, simultaneously condemning the violence perpetrated by both sides in the conflict.

Critiques of Camus's political views extended beyond the specific context of Algeria, delving into his overall engagement with politics. Some claimed that he displayed an apolitical stance or tried to avoid aligning himself with clear ideological positions. Critics argued that his philosophical beliefs, including his emphasis on individual freedom and the struggle against oppression, should have led him to actively participate in specific political movements or align himself with particular ideologies. However, Camus consistently asserted his independence from any particular political ideology, emphasising the importance of personal autonomy and critical thinking.

It is crucial to recognise that throughout his political engagements and writings, Camus remained steadfast in his concern for human dignity, his pursuit of justice, and his impulse to champion the rights of the oppressed. His commitment to delving into the complexities of political issues without blindly aligning with any doctrine or party aligned with his overall philosophical approach. Camus believed in the power of dialogue, empathy, and the examination of shared values as vehicles for reconciliation, even during intense conflicts.

The critiques and controversies surrounding Camus's political views reveal the intricacies of navigating political questions within a complex and ever-changing world. They also highlight the enduring relevance and ongoing discussion of his ideas, compelling readers and scholars alike to grapple with the complexities of political engagement and the pursuit of justice. Camus's ability to provoke thought and introspection in the realm of politics ensures that his contributions to these debates endure, providing a rich tapestry for future generations to explore and interpret. In an era marked by increasing polarisation and dogmatism, Camus's emphasis on critical thinking, empathy, and the pursuit of justice serves as a timeless reminder of the importance of intellectual independence and engagement with the political challenges of our time.

Twenty-Nine

Legacy and Contemporary Relevance

Albert Camus's legacy continues to resonate in the fields of philosophy and literature, making his work as relevant today as it was during his lifetime. His writings have left a lasting impact, influencing subsequent generations of thinkers, writers, and artists.

Camus's philosophy of absurdism remains a cornerstone of existential thought. Rooted in recognising the human tendency to seek meaning in an indifferent universe, Camus's exploration of the absurd has captivated readers for decades. The concept of the absurd sits at the core of his most famous work, "The Myth of Sisyphus," where he argues that existence is fundamentally irrational and devoid of predetermined meaning. Camus's approach challenges traditional philosophical perspectives that seek to establish objective truths and systems of thought to make sense of the world. Instead, he embraces the paradoxical nature of existence, celebrating the sometimes inexplicable and unpredictable experiences of being human.

Furthermore, Camus's ideas surrounding freedom, rebellion, and the pursuit of authenticity carry a timeless relevance. He challenges the constraining narratives imposed by society and advocates for individual autonomy as essential to the human experience. Camus famously declared, "I rebel, therefore we exist," asserting that rebellion against oppressive systems and injustices is not only a personal act but also a collective one that reaffirms the worth and agency of human beings. In our increasingly interconnected and complex world, Camus's call for personal responsibility and the rejection of conformity is a poignant reminder of the importance of staying true to oneself and resisting societal pressures.

Camus's literary style and narrative techniques have also left a lasting impact on the literary world. His ability to convey complex philosophical ideas through compelling storytelling has made him a figure of great admiration and influence among writers. Camus's concise and clear prose, powerful imagery, and evocative symbolism create a profound sense of engagement with his works. By seamlessly integrating philosophical and existential themes into narratives that resonate on both intellectual and emotional levels, Camus captures the reader's attention and invites them to grapple with the timeless questions of human existence.

In contemporary philosophy, Camus's ideas have been a touchstone in ongoing debates. Scholars and thinkers draw upon his works to explore subjects such as the nature of ethics, the role of human agency, and the complexities of morality. Camus's thoughts on the relationship between the individual and society continue to inform discussions on political philosophy. His emphasis on personal responsibility and his critique of totalitarian regimes remain particularly relevant in today's sociopolitical climate, where the struggle for individual freedom and the fight against oppressive systems persist.

Camus's engagement with political and social issues, particularly his vocal opposition to colonialism and his involvement in the Algerian War, further cements his contemporary relevance. Despite criticism for his perceived silence on certain issues or failure to fully interrogate power dynamics, Camus's unwavering commitment to justice, equality, and the rights of the marginalised continues to inspire activists and thinkers working towards social change. His writings on the complex relationship between oppressor and oppressed and his call for empathy and understanding remain significant contributions to the ongoing discourse on decolonisation, human rights, and collective responsibility.

Moreover, Camus's exploration of the "absurd hero" concept holds significant contemporary relevance. The absurd hero, exemplified by characters such as Meursault in "The Stranger," embodies a willingness to confront the absurdity of the human condition and find meaning within it. In a world plagued by uncertainty, existential crises, and moral dilemmas, Camus's depiction of the absurd hero offers solace and guidance. It encourages individuals to embrace their flawed and contradictory nature, to navigate the complexities of existence with an unwavering commitment to their own truth, and to defy the notion that life must have absolute meaning to be worthwhile.

Camus's writing style, characterised by its lucidity and elegance, inspires contemporary writers and intellectuals. His ability to engage readers through thought-provoking narratives and philosophical insights remains unparalleled. The existential themes he explores, such as the search for meaning, the pursuit of personal freedom, and the confrontation of mortality, resonate deeply with individuals grappling with the complexities of modern life. Camus's works continue to be read and studied in academic settings, where they serve as a foundation for understanding existentialism, absurdism, and the human condition.

In conclusion, Albert Camus's legacy is profoundly significant in philosophy and literature. His exploration of the absurd, the search for meaning, and the rejection of oppressive systems continue to resonate with readers and thinkers alike. Through his works, he challenges us to confront our existence, encourages us to find meaning and authenticity in an uncertain world, and reminds us of our power and responsibility to shape our lives. Camus's continued relevance speaks to the enduring appeal and continued relevance of his ideas, making him a figure whose contributions will be cherished and studied for generations.

THIRTY

THE ENDURING IMPACT OF CAMUS'S IDEAS AND WRITINGS

The enduring impact of Albert Camus's ideas and writings can be felt across various disciplines, from philosophy and literature to psychology, sociology, and beyond. His exploration of existentialism, absurdism, and the human condition has left an indelible mark on intellectual discourse and continues to inspire and challenge thinkers, writers, and activists today.

Camus's works, such as "The Stranger," "The Plague," "The Myth of Sisyphus," and "The Fall," delve deep into the profound questions that plague human existence. With his unique narrative style, Camus captures the essence of the human struggle, taking readers on a journey to confront fundamental doubts about the meaning of life and the rationality of the universe. Through his philosophical probes, he invites readers to explore the intricate relationship between freedom and responsibility, the tension between individual desires and collective obligations, and the role of rebellion in the face of absurdity.

Camus's understanding of the human condition was profoundly shaped by his time's social and political context. Witnessing the upheavals of the 20th century, including two world wars, the rise of totalitarianism, and the fight against colonialism, he confronted the darker aspects of human nature and the collective violence that permeates societies. His literary works reflect his commitment to social justice and his unwavering belief in the inherent dignity and worth of every human being.

One of Camus's essential contributions is his profound insight into the absurdity of human existence. He argued that the human desire for meaning and purpose often clashes with the indifferent and chaotic nature of the universe. In a world devoid of inherent meaning, individuals can accept the absurdity, embrace revolt, or succumb to despair and nihilism. Through the character of Meursault in "The Stranger," Camus illustrates the consequences of one's confrontation with the absurd, where the protagonist is alienated from society and ultimately sentenced to death, highlighting the tragic consequences of refusing to conform to societal expectations.

Camus's exploration of the absurd also resonates deeply with psychological and sociological research. In psychology, his writings have contributed to the understanding of existential angst and the search for meaning in life. His concept of the absurd aligns closely with existential psychology, which emphasises how individuals can find purpose and meaning through the subjective construction of their own lives. In sociology, his works offer insights into the alienating effects of modernity and how societal structures can contribute to the human experience of absurdity.

Beyond philosophy and social sciences, Camus's writings have left an indelible mark on literature and the arts. His minimalist writing style has inspired authors seeking to convey profound ideas through clear and concise prose. The evocative imagery in his works immerses readers in vivid emotional landscapes, enabling them to experience the complexity and ambiguity of the human condition firsthand. Camus's literary contributions have also resonated with filmmakers, playwrights, and visual artists who seek to capture the essence of human existence through various artistic forms.

Moreover, Camus's emphasis on revolt and resistance has been a source of inspiration for social and political activists. He believed in the power of individuals to challenge oppressive systems and fight for justice and freedom. His critique of totalitarianism and his unwavering commitment to human rights continue to resonate with those engaged in activism and social movements amidst ongoing struggles for equality, democracy, and social justice.

In the contemporary world, Camus's ideas remain relevant and critical guides for navigating the complexities of existence. As societies grapple with rising uncertainty, social fragmentation, and the erosion of values, his writings continue to provide insights into the human yearning for meaning, the importance of solidarity in the face of adversity, and the necessity for ethical action in an indifferent world.

In conclusion, the enduring impact of Albert Camus's ideas and writings continues reverberating across disciplines and generations. His exploration of existentialism, absurdism, and the human condition offers profound insights into the complexities of existence, inspiring readers to reflect on the fundamental questions of life. Through his literary works, Camus challenges us to confront the absurdities and injustices of the world and urges us to rebel against oppressive systems in the relentless pursuit of truth, justice, and compassion. His influence, both within academia and in the broader cultural landscape, is a testament to the enduring power of ideas and the transformative potential of literature and philosophy.

THIRTY-ONE

CAMUS'S RELEVANCE IN THE CONTEMPORARY PHILOSOPHICAL AND CULTURAL LANDSCAPE

In the vast philosophical and cultural landscape of the 21st century, the relevance of Albert Camus and his ideas stands as a formidable testament to the enduring search for meaning and purpose in human existence. Renowned as a writer of exceptional depth and insight, Camus's contributions to existentialism and absurdism have left an indelible mark on the collective consciousness of our time.

As we navigate the complexities of modern life, Camus's philosophy offers a necessary compass to guide us through the existential maze. At the core of his thinking is absurdism – the belief that the universe is fundamentally devoid of inherent meaning or purpose. Rather than descending into nihilism or resignation, Camus implores us to confront this absurdity head-on, encouraging us to embrace the freedom and agency that comes from recognising the inherent lack of meaning. Through the act of rebellion against absurdity, we can carve out our own individual meaning, reclaiming a sense of purpose in a seemingly indifferent universe.

Camus's philosophy takes on an added potency when considered against the backdrop of the 20th century, a time remorselessly marked by war, political turmoil, and existential crises. His experiences as a witness to the horrors of World War II and the subsequent struggle for justice and human rights deeply influenced his thinking. Camus believed that in the face of suffering and adversity, the only authentic response was to rebel against injustice actively, fight against the societal structures that perpetuate human suffering, and consistently uphold the principles of compassion and empathy. His unwavering insistence on the importance of individual responsibility in pursuing justice serves as a timely reminder in our turbulent times, where global challenges such as climate change, inequality, and oppression continue to test our collective humanity.

Moreover, Camus's literary works – his novels, essays, and plays – are treasures that offer profound insight into the human psyche. Through vivid character portrayals and searing descriptions, Camus delves into themes of alienation, isolation, and the eternal quest for meaning. In "The Stranger," Meursault's existential detachment and subsequent trial emphasise the disconnect between societal conventions and personal authenticity. In "The Plague," the fictional town of Oran becomes an allegory for the moral and existential crises humanity faces in the face of an epidemic. These narratives reflect the universal struggle of individuals seeking their place in a chaotic and unpredictable world, resonating deeply with readers seeking solace, understanding, and a sense of belonging.

To comprehend the full breadth of Camus's relevance, we must recognise his profound influence beyond academic and intellectual circles. His ideas have transcended the confines of philosophy, permeating various facets of artistic expression. Writers, musicians, filmmakers, and visual artists have drawn inspiration from Camus's works and ideas, incorporating his themes into their own creative endeavours. The universality of his exploration of the human experience has made him a beloved figure whose impact extends across cultures, languages, and generations.

In the midst of the current global landscape, characterised by political polarisation, societal fragmentation, and existential uncertainty, Camus's philosophy resonates with a heightened urgency. It compels us to introspection and self-reflection, urging us to critically evaluate our role in the world and our capacity for empathy and compassion. By embracing the absurdity of existence, we are encouraged to transcend the limitations imposed upon us by society, embrace our individual freedoms, and create meaningful lives. Camus's legacy serves as an enduring reminder that despite the inevitable trials and tribulations we face, it is within our power to shape our existence in a manner consistent with our humanistic values.

In conclusion, Albert Camus's and his ideas' relevance in the contemporary philosophical and cultural landscape remains palpable and profound. His concepts of absurdism, rebellion, and the pursuit of meaning form a vital framework for navigating the complexities of our existence. Against a backdrop of existential uncertainty and societal discord, his philosophy implores us to confront life's absurdity, act with responsibility and compassion, and strive for individual freedom in an indifferent universe. Camus's profound insights, coupled with his enduring influence on literature and the arts, ensure that his legacy will continue to captivate and inspire future generations.

Thirty-Two

Reflections on Camus's Influence in Current Philosophical Debates

Albert Camus's influence in current philosophical debates remains substantial, even decades after his death. His ideas and writings continue to provoke critical thought and engage with important questions about the nature of existence, morality, and the human condition.

One area where Camus's influence can be seen is existentialism and its variations. His concept of the absurd, which emphasises the inherent meaninglessness and paradoxes of human existence, has profoundly influenced contemporary existential thinkers. Camus's recognition of the absurdity of life challenges individuals to confront the ultimate futility of their actions, leading to a renewed exploration of the nature of authenticity and personal agency. By acknowledging the absurd, philosophers grapple with the tension between the desire for meaning and the reality of a universe that appears indifferent to human existence.

Existential philosophers inspired by Camus's philosophy have expanded upon his ideas, creating nuanced understandings of the absurd. Scholars like Jean-Paul Sartre and Simone de Beauvoir built upon Camus's concept of absurdity, delving into the complexities of freedom, responsibility, and the construction of meaning. Sartre's existentialism, for example, highlights the notion of individuals as "beings-for-itself" who are plagued by a constant search for identity and purpose in an inherently meaningless universe.

Furthermore, Camus's exploration of the human condition, through his portrayal of alienation, the tension between individual freedom and societal expectations, and the inevitability of suffering, remains relevant in contemporary philosophical debates. The notion of the "Other" and the complexities of identity, as depicted in Camus's novel "The Stranger," continue to stimulate discussions on the construction of self and the impact of societal norms on individual autonomy.

Intersectional feminism, for instance, draws upon Camus's examination of societal expectations and the struggle of marginalised voices within oppressive systems. Scholars in this field explore how gender, race, sexuality, and other intersecting identities intersect with existential questions of authenticity, freedom, and agency.

Camus's philosophy also offers insights into the nature of power, justice, and political engagement. His opposition to totalitarianism, emphasised in his essay "The Rebel," remains crucial in contemporary discussions on the dangers of ideological extremism and the erosion of democratic values. Camus challenges individuals to reassess their political beliefs and the potential consequences of blind adherence to dogma.

Moreover, his advocacy for political activism and commitment to justice serve as a powerful reminder of the importance of social engagement in the face of injustice and oppression. In the context of current socio-political movements, such as Black Lives Matter and environmental activism, scholars and activists draw from Camus's philosophy to reflect on the ethical responsibilities of individuals in combating systemic injustices and to inspire collective action.

In recent years, Camus's views on the ethics of violence and the absurdity of political violence have drawn renewed interest. His rejection of terrorism as a means of political struggle and his emphasis on the preservation of innocent lives resonate with contemporary debates on just warfare, the use of force in conflicts, and the moral implications of violence.

Contemporary scholars and activists explore Camus's insights on non-violent resistance and civil disobedience as they seek to address systemic issues and hierarchies without compromising the foundational principles of justice and compassion. The concept of engaging in peaceful forms of protest and resistance, rooted in Camus's philosophy, continues to shape popular movements worldwide.

Camus's notion of the absurd hero, someone who defiantly confronts the absurdity of existence and embraces a rebellious spirit, has also found resonance in contemporary discussions on personal autonomy, self-determination, and individual agency. His philosophy encourages individuals to boldly face the seemingly meaningless aspects of life and assert their freedom in the face of adversity and existential challenges.

Moreover, Camus's writings continue to inspire literary and artistic works, showcasing his enduring influence on various forms of creative expression. Filmmakers, playwrights, and musicians often draw inspiration from his themes and ideas, reimagining them in contemporary contexts and exploring their relevance to current social and psychological dilemmas.

Through artistic interpretations, Camus's philosophy reaches a wider audience and stimulates further discussion and reflection on the complexities of existence.

Overall, Camus's influence in current philosophical debates is a testament to the timeless relevance of his ideas. By addressing fundamental questions about the human condition, morality, and the search for meaning, his works continue to stimulate critical thinking and engage with contemporary issues.

As new generations of thinkers and artists discover his writings, Camus's legacy as a philosophical icon lives on, shaping and enriching current debates and inspiring individuals to delve deeply into the complexities of existence.

THIRTY-THREE

CONCLUSION

Albert Camus left an indelible mark on literature and existential philosophy throughout his life and work. Born in French Algeria, Camus's journey began in a politically charged environment that would greatly influence his worldview and shape his literary and philosophical endeavours.

Growing up in poverty, Camus experienced first-hand the deep inequalities and prejudices that plagued the colonial society of his time. This deeply ingrained sense of social injustice would later manifest in his writing and activism as he became a fierce advocate for human rights and a vocal critic of oppressive systems.

Camus's literary journey began in his late teens when he started writing for local newspapers and literary magazines. During this time, he developed his unique style, characterised by its lucidity, precision, and clarity. His love for language and storytelling allowed him to craft emotionally and intellectually engaging narratives, drawing readers into his profound philosophical enquiries.

In 1942, Camus published his first major novel, "The Stranger," which introduced readers to his philosophical concept of the absurd. The story follows Meursault, a detached and indifferent protagonist who becomes embroiled in an unforeseen event, leading to his moral and existential awakening. Through Meursault's experiences, Camus explores the themes of alienation, the futility of human existence, and the inevitability of death.

"The Stranger" resonates deeply with readers due to its unsettling portrayal of the human condition. Meursault's indifference and apathy challenge conventional notions of morality and invite contemplation on the nature of individual freedom and the meaning of life. As Camus famously said, "In the depths of winter, I finally learnt that within me there lay an invincible summer." This sentiment captures the essence of his philosophy, suggesting that even in the face of absurdity and suffering, one can find inner strength and purpose.

In 1947, Camus published "The Plague," a novel set in Oran, depicting a fictional town devastated by an outbreak of the bubonic plague. The narrative serves as an allegory for the human condition, examining the widespread suffering, existential despair, and the choices individuals make when faced with the absurdity of mortality. This work further solidified Camus's position as an existential thinker and brought him international recognition.

"The Plague" became a reflection on the horrors of the Second World War, resonating with a world still grappling with the aftermath of such widespread destruction. Through the characters in the novel, Camus explores the fragility of human existence, the moral responsibility of individuals to confront the absurd, and the potential for solidarity and compassion in the face of adversity. It serves as a haunting reminder of the power of collective action and the role of the individual in shaping their own destiny.

Camus's philosophical treatise, "The Myth of Sisyphus," published in 1942, delves deep into the notion of the absurd. Drawing inspiration from Greek mythology, Camus presents Sisyphus, condemned to roll a boulder uphill for eternity, as a metaphor for the human condition. Through this metaphor, Camus suggests that life's struggles and the quest for meaning are ultimately fruitless. Yet, true freedom and purpose can be found through the act of rebellion and acceptance of this existential absurdity.

"The Myth of Sisyphus" delves into the philosophical questions that have haunted humanity for centuries. It challenges traditional notions of happiness and invites readers to confront the inherent purposelessness of existence while urging them to embrace life's fleeting moments of joy and the potential for personal growth and transformation. Camus suggests that we can reach a state of contentment and authenticity by accepting the absurd and creating our own individual meaning.

In "The Fall," published in 1956, Camus explores the themes of guilt, judgement, and hypocrisy through the confessions of the narrator, Jean-Baptiste Clamence. The novel invites readers to ponder the moral complexities of human nature, challenging individuals to confront their own shortcomings and question their preconceived notions of morality.

"The Fall" delves into the moral ambiguities that exist within each of us. Clamence's introspective and candid confessions force readers to confront their own potential for judgment and self-deception. Through Clamence's revelations, Camus reminds us of the fragility of our moral certainties and highlights the importance of self-reflection and empathy as we navigate the complexities of the human experience.

His fervent activism accompanied Camus's literary achievements. He was an active member of the French Resistance during World War II, using his writing and journalistic skills to propagate resistance propaganda. After the war, he became involved in numerous political causes, advocating for peace and justice in a post-war world ravaged by violence and totalitarian ideologies.

Camus's activism reflected his unwavering commitment to justice and human rights. He criticised both the totalitarian regimes of his time, including Stalinism and fascism, and the inherent inequalities of the capitalist system. Camus believed writers and intellectuals had a moral duty to use their platform to bring positive societal change.

Despite the controversies surrounding his political views, Camus's contributions to philosophy and literature remain significant. His refusal to accept a world without meaning and insistence on the importance of individual freedom continues to inspire thinkers and writers today. His concept of the absurd hero, someone who confronts the absurdity of existence with rebellion, resonates with those who question societal norms and seek personal authenticity.

Camus's impact extended beyond his literary and philosophical pursuits. He dedicated himself to promoting dialogue between different cultures and advocated for peace in the face of escalating tensions between various nations during the Cold War era. Camus emphasised the fundamental humanity that connects all individuals, irrespective of their cultural or ideological differences.

In conclusion, Albert Camus's writings delve deeply into the human condition, providing profound insights into the absurdity of life and the pursuit of meaning and authenticity. His impact on literature, philosophy, and cultural discourse is undeniable, and his ideas continue to provoke thought and inspire exploration into the complexities of the human experience. As a writer and activist, Camus's profound understanding of the human condition and his unwavering commitment to social justice serve as a testament to the enduring power of literature to illuminate the fundamental truths of existence. His legacy reminds us that we can strive to create a more just and meaningful world through art, philosophy, and activism.

Thirty-Four

Summarising Camus's Contributions to Philosophy and Literature

Albert Camus is widely regarded as one of the most influential thinkers of the 20th century. Born on November 7, 1913, in Mondovi, Algeria, Camus experienced a tumultuous childhood. His father died in World War I when Camus was just one year old, leaving his mother to raise him and his older brother alone. This early experience of loss and hardship would later shape Camus's existential thinking and exploration of the human condition.

Camus's early literary aspirations were apparent from a young age. He began writing and publishing articles in local newspapers, cultivating his craft while working as a journalist. His exposure to the diverse cultural milieu of

Algeria, with its blend of French, Arab, and Berber influences, expanded his perspectives and laid the foundation for his later works.

Camus began his formal education at the University of Algiers, where he studied philosophy. During these formative years, he developed a keen interest in the works of Friedrich Nietzsche and Jean-Paul Sartre. Nietzsche's ideas about individualism, rebellion, and the pursuit of self-realisation resonated deeply with Camus. Sartre's existentialist philosophy and exploration of freedom and responsibility greatly influenced Camus's thinking. This intellectual nourishment would become instrumental in developing his unique philosophical and literary voice.

In 1942, Camus published his first major philosophical work, "The Myth of Sisyphus." This essay captured the essence of his thought, dissecting the human desire for meaning in a world that seems devoid of inherent purpose. Camus introduced the notion of the absurd, asserting that life's fundamental contradictions make it inherently absurd. He grappled with the question of whether one should embrace this absurdity or search for meaning despite its apparent absence.

Camus explored these existential themes in his novels, such as "The Stranger" and "The Plague." In "The Stranger," Camus presents the enigmatic character of Meursault, who symbolises the disenchanted individual navigating a seemingly indifferent world. Through Meursault's apathetic demeanour and ultimate rejection of society's moral codes, Camus interrogates the nature of existential freedom and personal responsibility.

"The Plague," considered one of Camus's masterpieces, delves into the philosophical and psychological implications of a fictional town's struggle with a devastating epidemic. The novel is a powerful allegory for the human condition, representing the absurdity of life through the plague's relentless and indiscriminate assault on the town's inhabitants. Camus uses this existential crisis to explore themes of solidarity, rebellion, and the ultimate triumph of the human spirit in the face of overwhelming adversity.

Camus's philosophical and literary endeavours were not confined to fiction. He tackled various social and political issues in his essays and speeches. Camus staunchly opposed both communism and colonialism, criticising the oppressive regimes that perpetuated these ideologies. His unwavering commitment to individual freedom and human rights earned him admiration among those who sought to challenge oppressive systems.

However, his outspoken beliefs also garnered criticism and controversy. Camus's disagreements with Jean-Paul Sartre, who aligned himself with communism, led to a prominent ideological rift between the two intellectuals. This clash further solidified Camus's reputation as an independent thinker and an advocate for personal freedom and authenticity.

On January 4, 1960, at the age of 46, Camus's life was tragically cut short. He died in a car accident, leaving a void in the literary and philosophical world. Nevertheless, his ideas and contributions continue to resonate with readers and thinkers around the globe.

Camus's profound influence on literature and philosophy endures. His exploration of the absurdity of existence challenges readers to confront the human condition honestly and without illusion. Through his works, Camus invites us to question societal expectations, grapple with the contradictions of life, and assert our freedom in the face of indifference.

Today, Camus's legacy remains vibrant. His ideas have inspired subsequent generations of writers, artists, and thinkers to engage with existential and philosophical questions. His works continue to be studied and discussed in academic circles, illuminating the complexities and paradoxes of the human experience. Camus's insights into the human condition offer solace and guidance to those navigating the intricacies of contemporary life, urging individuals to find meaning in the face of adversity.

In conclusion, Albert Camus's contributions to philosophy and literature transcend time and continue to captivate readers and thinkers alike. His exploration of the absurdity of existence, coupled with his unwavering commitment to individual freedom and authenticity, has left an indelible mark on intellectual discourse. Through his works, Camus challenges us to confront life's inherent contradictions, find meaning in the face of adversity, and forge our own path in an often perplexing world.

Thirty-Five

Reflecting on the Complexities and Nuances of His Legacy

Albert Camus left behind a rich and complex legacy that continues to captivate readers, philosophers, and literary enthusiasts today. His works, which explore themes of absurdity, the human condition, and morality, challenge our perceptions and provoke deep introspection. However, as we reflect on Camus's legacy, it is important to recognise the intricacies and nuances that make his contributions to philosophy and literature both compelling and controversial.

One of the central complexities of Camus's legacy lies in his philosophical position of absurdism. The idea that life is inherently meaningless and absurd yet should be lived with passion and rebellion continues to resonate with many readers. Camus suggests that individuals must confront the absurdity of existence and create their own meaning, all while acknowledging that this pursuit is ultimately futile. This existential framework has drawn admiration and inspiration from countless individuals who find solace in Camus's call to embrace the absurdity of life.

However, as with any philosophical standpoint, there are criticisms and counterarguments. Some argue that Camus's emphasis on the absurd ignores the potential for a meaningful existence and overlooks the importance of finding purpose and fulfilment. Critics contend that his philosophy may lead to nihilism, as it seemingly rejects the possibility of objective meaning and dismisses the importance of values and ethics. This nuanced debate surrounding the proper response to the absurdity of life is a key aspect of Camus's legacy, reflecting the enduring nature of philosophical discourse.

Another nuance of Camus's legacy lies in his engagement with politics and social issues of his time. Although he is often celebrated as a voice for justice and humanism, controversies surround his stance on colonialism and the Algerian War. Camus's support for the French Algerian community during the war has been criticised for failing to align his principles with the struggle for Algerian independence. This aspect of his legacy raises questions about the role of intellectuals in political movements and the complexities of navigating conflicting ideals.

Camus's complex relationship with the French Resistance during World War II further adds to the intricacy of his legacy. While he became involved in the fight against Nazi occupation and used his writing to support the Resistance, some have questioned the sincerity and consistency of his actions. Critics argue that Camus never fully committed to the Resistance and that his involvement was more performative than genuine. This controversy underscores the challenges individuals face navigating political movements and the complexities of authenticity and moral obligation.

In addition to these political complexities, Camus's literary style contributes to the depth of his legacy. His writings, characterised by concise prose and vivid descriptions, have profoundly affected modern literature. Camus's ability to encapsulate complex philosophical ideas in compelling narratives has inspired countless authors to experiment with form and language. His impact extends beyond content and into the realm of style and craft, influencing generations of writers and solidifying his place in the literary canon.

Furthermore, Camus's legacy extends beyond his philosophical and literary contributions. His Nobel Prize for Literature in 1957 recognised his remarkable literary achievements and affirmed his importance in the world of letters. This prestigious accolade solidified his place in the canon of great writers, further cementing the impact of his work on future generations of readers and thinkers.

Camus's ideas remain relevant and thought-provoking in today's philosophical and cultural landscape. Exploring the absurdity of existence, the quest for personal meaning, and the examination of moral responsibility are perennial topics that continue to engage scholars and readers alike. Camus's legacy reminds us of the enduring power of literature and philosophy to challenge, inspire, and shape our understanding of the world.

In conclusion, reflecting on the complexities and nuances of Albert Camus's legacy reveals his ideas' enduring relevance and impact. From his exploration of the absurdity of life to his engagement with social and political issues, Camus's contributions to philosophy and literature have sparked profound discussions and debates. While his philosophy may be subject to critique, there is no doubt that Camus's legacy continues to enrich our understanding of the human condition and encourages us to grapple with the complexities of existence. His involvement in political movements, his literary style, and the recognition of his literary achievements further contribute to the multidimensionality of his legacy. Albert Camus remains an influential figure, inspiring generations of readers and serving as a reminder of the profound intersections of philosophy, literature, and human experience.

Thirty-Six

Appendix

In the appendix to this book, you will find a wealth of additional resources and information that delve deeper into Albert Camus's life, works, and philosophical concepts. This expanded section includes a comprehensive timeline of key events in Camus's life, an extensive glossary of important terms and concepts found in his writings, a rich compilation of suggested readings for further exploration, and an analysis of his literary style and impact on contemporary literature.

Timeline of Albert Camus's Life:

- 1913: Albert Camus is born on November 7 in Mondovi, French Algeria, into a humble working-class family. He grew up witnessing the disparities and injustices of colonial Algeria, which deeply influenced his later writings and political views.

- 1930s: Camus diligently studies philosophy at the University of Algiers while immersing himself in the city's vibrant cultural scene. He becomes involved in theatre and journalism, developing critical thinking skills and a flair for writing. His early literary works laid the foundation for his future philosophy, grappling with themes of alienation, rebellion, and the absurd.

- 1942: Camus publishes his first major philosophical work, "The Myth of Sisyphus." In this profound essay, he explores the concept of the absurd and its implications for the human condition. Camus argues that embracing the absurdity of existence leads to genuine freedom and the possibility of creating meaning in life.

- 1942-1943: During World War II, Camus joins the French Resistance, engaging in covert activities against the Nazi occupation in France. His experiences during this time shaped his views on rebellion, justice, and the struggle against oppressive forces. Camus's involvement in the Resistance solidifies his commitment to ethical principles and his conviction that individuals must act against injustice.

- 1947: Camus's novel "The Plague" is published, offering a gripping and allegorical account of a plague-infested town. This work propelled him to international recognition, and he received critical acclaim for exploring human resilience in the face of suffering and death. "The Plague" reflects Camus's philosophical ideas and his belief in the possibility of finding meaning and solidarity amid the absurd and tragic aspects of life.

- 1951: Camus publishes his seminal work, "The Rebel," in which he delves deeply into the complex issues of rebellion, morality, and the role of the individual in society. With incisive critiques of authoritarian regimes and revolutionary movements, Camus proposes a path that balances justice and freedom. This work sparks intense discussions and debates, establishing Camus as a leading political and philosophical discourse voice.

- 1956: As the Algerian War for Independence intensified, Camus expressed his opposition to French colonialism and the methods used by the Algerian independence movement. His position places him in a delicate predicament where he fiercely advocates for human rights and justice while navigating the complexities of the conflict. Camus's stance on the Algerian War alienates some of his intellectual peers and contributes to a divide in public opinion.

- 1960: On January 4, Camus delivers his Nobel Prize acceptance speech, emphasising the values of courage, integrity, and human solidarity. Tragically, ten days later, on January 14, Camus lost his life in a car accident near Sens, France. The literary world mourns the loss of a genius who had fearlessly confronted the human condition and offered profound reflections on morality and the meaning of life.

Glossary of Key Terms and Concepts:

- Absurdism: Camus's philosophical concept that life and the universe are inherently without meaning or purpose and that humans must confront the inherent absurdity of their existence. By accepting the absurd, individuals can find authenticity and purpose in taking responsibility for their actions. Absurdism challenges traditional notions of meaning and invites individuals to create their own subjective meaning in a seemingly meaningless world.

- Existentialism: A philosophical movement that emphasises individual freedom and responsibility while rejecting external authority and predetermined meaning. Camus aligns with some existentialist ideas but criticises the movement's tendency to overlook the importance of social and political dimensions. For Camus, existentialism must confront the contradictions and demands of both individual existence and collective responsibility.

- Absurd hero: The Camusian notion of a hero who confronts the absurdity of existence with rebellion, embracing life's challenges despite the lack of inherent or universal meaning. The absurd hero's defiance and consciousness exemplify their quest for integrity, and they refuse to succumb to the absurd. Camus's protagonists, such as Meursault in "The Stranger," embody the absurd hero, facing life's absurdity and finding a genuine sense of purpose and authenticity.

- Rebellion: Camus's belief in the inherent value of resisting and rebelling against unjust systems and oppressive forces. Rebellion demands recognising one's freedom and dignity, ultimately aiming at creating a just and meaningful world. For Camus, true rebellion requires a personal and collective commitment to justice, recognising the complex interplay between individual agency and societal structures.

- Guilt: A moral and psychological state explored by Camus, often tied to themes of responsibility, judgement, and the consequences of our actions. He distinguishes between guilt that arises from genuine transgressions and the manipulation of guilt as a form of control and oppression. Camus questions the constructive potential of guilt and encourages individuals to take responsibility for their actions without being burdened or manipulated by unfounded guilt.

Analysis of Camus's Literary Style and Impact on Contemporary Literature:

Albert Camus is renowned for his elegant and lyrical prose skillfully combines philosophical ideas with compelling narratives, engaging readers on multiple levels. His writing style is characterised by clarity and conciseness, allowing complex concepts to be conveyed in accessible language. Camus's ability to create vivid and evocative descriptions immerses readers in the worlds he constructs, whether the blistering Algerian sun or the hauntingly desolate streets of a plague-ridden town.

Camus's works have profoundly impacted contemporary literature, philosophy, and popular culture. His exploration of existential themes, such as alienation, the absurd, and the search for personal meaning, resonates with readers across generations. Camus's writings challenge conventional wisdom and invite profound introspection, encouraging readers to confront the essential questions of human existence and society's capacity for good and evil.

Furthermore, Camus's philosophy and literary works continue to inspire contemporary authors and thinkers who engage with questions of ethics, justice, and the human condition. His emphasis on the importance of individual freedom, rebellion against injustice, and the search for authentic meaning remains relevant in discussions surrounding political activism, social justice movements, and personal identity.

In conclusion, the appendix of this book provides a comprehensive compilation of resources to explore Albert Camus's life, ideas, and literary contributions further. By following the suggested readings, considering the glossary of key terms, and reflecting on Camus's impact on literature and philosophy, readers can deepen their understanding of this renowned writer's legacy and the enduring relevance of his work in an ever-changing world.

Timeline of Albert Camus's Life

Albert Camus is born on November 7, 1913, in Mondovi, a small coastal town in French Algeria. His parents, Lucien Camus and Catherine Sintès belong to the working class, and the family resides in a poor neighbourhood in Algiers. Camus's upbringing is marked by hardships, including his father's death in World War I when Albert was just one year old, leaving his mother to raise him and his older brother on her own. Catherine, a house cleaner who is illiterate, instils in her sons a strong sense of values and a deep appreciation for education.

Despite their modest circumstances, Camus's mother provides him a primary education. In 1923, he entered a local secondary school, where he quickly distinguished himself as an exceptional student. Camus's academic prowess is matched only by his insatiable appetite for literature and philosophy. He devours the works of

Friedrich Nietzsche, Jean-Paul Sartre, Arthur Rimbaud, and other esteemed writers, forming a rich intellectual foundation at an early age. These readings fuel his growing rebellion against societal norms and the repressive colonial system surrounding him.

In 1930, at the age of 17, Camus left Algeria for France to pursue further education at the University of Algiers. He immerses himself in studying philosophy, delving into the works of classical and modern thinkers, including René Descartes, Immanuel Kant, and Henri Bergson. During this period, he encountered the philosophies of existentialism and absurdism, which laid the groundwork for his later works. Camus embraces these philosophical ideas, grappling with questions of human existence, morality, and the search for meaning in an indifferent universe.

In 1935, Camus completed his thesis on Plotinus, a significant figure in Neoplatonist philosophy, and graduated with a degree in philosophy. In the same year, he becomes involved in theatre activities and joins a group of young artists and intellectuals who question the prevailing values of their time. Camus's involvement in artistic circles exposes him to a breadth of perspectives and artistic expressions, further enriching his own creative spirit.

While still in university, Camus begins writing for "Alger Républicain," a left-wing newspaper committed to political and social justice. As a journalist, he covers many topics, including colonialism, poverty, and social inequality. His writing reflects his growing concern for the marginalised and his commitment to highlighting their struggles. Through his journalistic endeavours, Camus hones his craft, mastering the art of storytelling and developing a distinct writing style.

In 1942, Camus published his first major philosophical essay, "The Myth of Sisyphus," marking a pivotal moment in his career. This groundbreaking work explores the concept of the absurd—a central theme that permeates much of his later writings. Camus asserts that life is devoid of inherent meaning or purpose, highlighting the apparent futility of human existence. However, rather than succumbing to nihilism or despair, he posits that individuals can find meaning through a rebellious embrace of life's absurdity.

During World War II, Camus actively participates in the French Resistance, risking his life as a writer and editor for underground newspapers, including the renowned "Combat." His experiences within the Resistance expose him firsthand to the atrocities of war and the struggle against oppression. This period deeply informs his outlook on human dignity, justice, and freedom, laying the foundation for his moral and political perspectives.

In 1946, Camus published his most famous novel, "The Stranger" (originally titled "L'Étranger"). Through the story of Meursault, a detached and indifferent protagonist who inadvertently commits murder, Camus explores themes of existentialism, isolation, and the absurdity of human existence. The novel resonates with readers worldwide, captivating them with its stark portrayal of the human condition.

Camus's literary journey continues with the 1947 production of his play, "Caligula," a thought-provoking examination of the destructive nature of absolute power and tyranny. Drawing inspiration from the Roman emperor, Camus explores philosophical questions surrounding morality, freedom, and the consequences of nihilism. His ability to interweave social and political commentary with thoughtful introspection further solidifies his reputation as a profound and multifaceted thinker.

The same year, Camus published another seminal work, "The Plague" (originally titled "La Peste"). Set in the fictional Algerian town of Oran, the novel metaphorically reflects on the collective struggle against oppression and the human response to a deadly epidemic. Camus delves into questions of individual autonomy, social responsibility, and the potential for heroism in the face of adversity. "The Plague" solidifies Camus's place as a moralist and humanist, resonating deeply with readers navigating the complexities of post-war existence.

In 1951, Camus published his philosophical treatise, "The Rebel" (originally titled "L'Homme révolté"). Building on his earlier works, Camus examines the nature of rebellion and freedom, critiquing both communist and fascist ideologies that sacrifice human dignity. He advocates for a humanistic form of rebellion grounded in compassion and individual moral responsibility. "The Rebel" presents a profound critique of the totalitarian regimes of his time while offering a hopeful vision of human agency and moral integrity.

Camus's immense contributions to literature and philosophy were recognised in 1957 when he received the Nobel Prize in Literature. The prestigious award commends his "important literary production, which, with clear-sighted earnestness, lights up the problems of the human conscience in our time." The accolade solidifies his place among the great thinkers and writers of the 20th century and introduces a broader audience to his profound insights into the human condition.

Tragically, on January 4, 1959, Albert Camus's life is cut short in a car accident near Sens, France, at the age of 46. His untimely passing leaves a void in the literary world. Still, his legacy endured, carried forward by his extensive work and his impact on subsequent generations of writers, philosophers, and social critics.

In the years following his death, several collections of Camus's notebooks and unpublished works are published, shedding further light on his intellectual evolution and providing a deeper understanding of his unfinished projects. These posthumous writings explore his personal reflections, artistic endeavours, and thoughts on the persistent themes of his work. Camus's intellectual legacy continues to captivate and provoke new generations through these insights, ensuring his role as a paramount figure in the literary and philosophical landscape.

Glossary of Key Terms and Concepts in Camus's Work

In order to fully grasp the depth and complexity of Albert Camus's work and philosophy, it is essential to delve into some key terms and concepts that he frequently explores. This comprehensive glossary aims to provide thorough definitions and in-depth explanations of these important ideas, shedding light on their significance within Camus's body of work.

Absurdism - At the core of Camus's philosophy, absurdism refers to the belief that human existence is fundamentally irrational and devoid of any inherent meaning or purpose. Camus argues that individuals must confront the inherent absurdity of life and still seek meaning and purpose, creating their own values in the face of a chaotic and indifferent universe. Absurdism challenges the notion of a fixed and objective reality, advocating for subjective interpretation and individual choice.

Existentialism - A philosophical movement that emphasises the individual's responsibility in creating their own existence and finding meaning in the world. Camus is often associated with existentialism, although he developed his own unique perspective within the broader framework. While existentialism explores the possibilities of human freedom and choice, Camus's philosophy also grapples with the limits and challenges imposed by the absurd. Existentialism confronts the inherent anxiety and anguish stemming from the individual's freedom to create their own values and the responsibility that accompanies it.

The Absurd - The concept of the absurd lies at the heart of Camus's philosophy. It refers to the inherent tension and contradiction between humanity's natural desire for meaning and the fundamental meaninglessness of existence. Camus argues that individuals should not succumb to despair or nihilism but embrace the absurd and find personal significance and fulfilment. Through this embrace and the search for authenticity, one can navigate the human condition. The absurd does not deny the existence of value or importance in life but rather challenges rigid systems of meaning and calls for a continuous questioning of one's existence.

Absurd Hero - Camus introduces the inspirational figure of the absurd hero as someone who rebels against the world's meaninglessness while fully aware of its absurdity. The absurd hero does not seek external validation or impose universal values but faces the absurdity with courage, authenticity, and a commitment to creating their own values. Rejecting blind conformity, the absurd hero takes responsibility for their actions, finding fulfilment in the act of rebellion against the absurd. The absurd hero embodies the human capability for revolt, asserting individual freedom in the face of an indifferent world.

Rebellion - Camus views rebellion as a vital response to the absurdity of existence. To rebel is to assert one's individuality and freedom actively, choosing one's own actions and beliefs in the face of an indifferent and irrational universe. Through rebellion, individuals resist the tendency to conform to societal norms and challenge oppressive systems. Rebellion is not limited to physical acts but encompasses a mental and philosophical stance, a refusal to accept the status quo and an unwavering commitment to personal authenticity. Through rebellion, individuals confront the absurd and affirm their existence in an otherwise indifferent world.

The Stranger - Considered one of Camus's most influential works, "The Stranger" explores the theme of absurdity through the story of its protagonist, Meursault. The novel investigates the isolation and indifference of human existence, society's reaction to those who refuse to conform, and the consequences of living a life unburdened by societal expectations. Through Meursault's detached and unconventional outlook on life, Camus portrays the absurdity of human existence and the resulting tension when faced with societal expectations that demand conformity. "The Stranger" challenges traditional moral judgements and invites readers to question the consequences of blind conformity.

Another monumental work by Camus, "The Plague," serves as a metaphor for the human condition and the struggle against a deadly epidemic. The novel reflects on the nature of suffering, individuals' choices under extreme circumstances, and the search for meaning in the face of tragedy. Through the stark portrayal of the plague's impact on society, Camus explores themes of heroism, solidarity, and the resilience of the human spirit. "The Plague" forces readers to confront the fragility of human existence, the absurdity of death, and the possibility of finding meaning and purpose even in the face of overwhelming adversity.

The Myth of Sisyphus - A philosophical essay by Camus, "The Myth of Sisyphus," delves into the idea of the absurd through the Greek mythological figure Sisyphus. Camus argues that Sisyphus's eternal task of rolling a boulder up a hill, only for it to roll back down inevitably, mirrors human existence's futility and repetitive nature. However, Camus also emphasises that we must imagine Sisyphus happy, as he finds meaning and purpose in the act of defiance against an indifferent universe. "The Myth of Sisyphus" explores the tension between the absurdity of existence and the human desire for happiness, emphasising that even in the face of an absurd life, there is the potential for finding joy and fulfilment.

Guilt and Judgement - Camus explores the themes of guilt and judgement in his novel "The Fall." The book delves into the moral complexities of human actions, the consequences of guilt, and the burden of self-judgement and hypocrisy. Through the character of Jean-Baptiste Clamence, a former lawyer who grapples with guilt, Camus highlights the fallibility of the human condition and the intricate web of moral choices we each face. "The Fall" urges readers to reflect on their own complicity and confront personal responsibility in a morally ambiguous world. It challenges conventional notions of guilt, emphasising the inherent complexities of human nature and the need for honest self-reflection.

These terms and concepts, among others prevalent in Camus's work, form the foundation of his philosophy. Engaging with these ideas allows readers to navigate the intricate web of existential questions Camus poses and delve deeper into the complexities of the human condition. By exploring the depths of absurdism, existentialism, rebellion, and the confrontation of the absurd, readers can develop a profound understanding of Camus's philosophy and its relevance in their lives.

Post-Scriptum

Few writers in the rich world of literature have captivated readers and prompted deep self-reflection as effectively as Albert Camus. Born in French Algeria, Camus became widely celebrated for his talents as a novelist, playwright, and essayist. Moreover, he emerged as a significant figure in the philosophical movement known as Existentialism.

Camus' childhood was marked by tragedy and hardship. His father died in battle during World War I when Camus was just a year old, leaving his mother alone to provide for him and his older brother Lucien. Struggling through poverty, Camus developed a deep empathy for the dispossessed and marginalised, a sentiment that would permeate much of his later work.

As a student at the University of Algiers, Camus excelled in his studies, delving into philosophy, literature, and journalism. He discovered the works of Friedrich Nietzsche,

Friedrich Hölderlin, and Fyodor Dostoevsky, whose writings would play a significant role in shaping his philosophical worldview. The themes of individual freedom, moral responsibility, and the absurdity of human existence resonated deeply with Camus and laid the foundation for his existentialist philosophy.

As a philosophical school of thought, existentialism asserts that individuals create meaning and purpose through their actions and choices. It rejects the notion of an objective and predetermined destiny, instead emphasising personal freedom and the responsibility that comes with it. Camus would later become associated with the branch of existentialism known as Absurdism, which acknowledges the inherent tension between the human desire for meaning and the impossibility of finding any transcendent purpose in a seemingly indifferent universe.

Camus' most famous works, "The Stranger" and "The Plague," exemplify his existentialist beliefs and explore the human condition in the face of absurdity and suffering. "The Stranger" tells the story of Meursault, a detached and apathetic protagonist who unwittingly commits a senseless murder. Through Meursault's journey toward self-realisation and societal condemnation, Camus portrays the existential predicament of an individual trapped between the search for meaning and the absurdity of existence.

In "The Plague," Camus explores the moral and philosophical implications of an epidemic that ravages the fictional town of Oran. As the citizens of Oran grapple with the existential crisis of a seemingly indifferent and unfair universe, the novel becomes not only a portrayal of the physical and emotional suffering caused by the plague but also an allegory for the wider human condition.

Beyond his fiction, Camus also contributed extensively through his philosophical essays, such as "The Myth of Sisyphus" and "The Rebel." In "The Myth of Sisyphus," Camus argues that life is characterised by a fundamental absurdity, likening human existence to the futile and repetitive task assigned to the Greek mythological figure, Sisyphus. Despite the inherent meaninglessness of life, Camus suggests that embracing the struggle and the realisation of the absurd can lead to a profound sense of rebellion and freedom.

"The Rebel," on the other hand, delves into the concept of revolt against injustice and oppression. Camus explores the ethical dimensions of rebellion, advocating for a balance between the desire for freedom and the recognition of the moral responsibility that accompanies it. He criticises both blind submission to authority and violent revolution, advocating instead for a humanistic and compassionate revolt that upholds justice and acknowledges the inherent dignity of all individuals.

Camus' unique existentialist perspective diverged from the more pessimistic views of his contemporary Jean-Paul Sartre. While both writers explored the themes of existential freedom and the human dilemma, Camus believed in the importance of individual morality and the pursuit of justice amidst the inherent absurdity of existence. This philosophical divergence would eventually strain their friendship and lead to a parting of ways.

As an artist and thinker, Camus left an indelible mark on the literary and philosophical landscape of the 20th century. His exploration of the absurdity of human existence and a deep commitment to moral and ethical values continue to resonate with readers and thinkers worldwide. Through his rich body of work, Albert Camus invites us to confront our own existential dilemmas, embrace the freedom to create meaning, and ultimately face the inherent absurdity of life with courage and integrity.

Due to their complexity and depth, Camus' writings have often sparked heated debates and interpretations. Critics have grappled with whether Camus was a true existentialist or his philosophy can be categorised under a specific label. While some argue that he remained faithful to the existentialist principles of individual freedom and responsibility, others point to his distinct emphasis on morality and the rejection of nihilism, which sets him apart from other existentialist thinkers.

Moreover, Camus' Algerian origins and his experiences of growing up in a colonial society deeply influenced his philosophical and political views. At a time of intense political and social unrest, his writings advocated for justice, compassion, and the recognition of the rights and dignity of all individuals. Camus' commitment to social justice led him to critique both the Western colonial powers and the nationalist movements, offering a unique perspective that sought to transcend the binary oppositions of the time.

In addition to his literary achievements, Camus was also an active participant in the French Resistance during World War II, fighting against Nazi occupation and collaborating with underground newspapers. However, his involvement with the Resistance and subsequent controversial political positions put him under scrutiny and faced accusations from both the left and the right.

Despite the controversies surrounding his life and work, Albert Camus remains an indomitable figure in the realm of literature and philosophy. His profound insights into the human condition, his courageous commitment to justice and freedom, and his exploration of the limits and possibilities of existence continue to inspire readers and thinkers across generations. In a world that often seems absurd and filled with suffering, Camus' writings remind us of the importance of embracing our individual autonomy, living with moral integrity, and finding meaning in the face of the inherent absurdity of life.

In philosophy, one name stands tall when exploring the concept of the absurd: Albert Camus. Camus, a renowned French philosopher and writer, delved deeply into the notion of the absurd in his works, notably in his novel The Stranger, published in 1942. Through his examination of the absurd, Camus contributed significantly to the development of existentialism. This philosophical movement emphasises individual existence and the meaning that humans create in a seemingly meaningless world.

The Stranger is a prime example of Camus's exploration of the absurd. The protagonist, Meursault, is an indifferent and detached individual who confronts life's unpredictable and often absurd events. The novel's opening line, "Mother died today," exemplifies the indifferent and matter-of-fact tone that pervades much of Meursault's narration. This depiction of an individual who fails to conform to societal expectations and norms resonates with Camus's concept of the absurd.

At the heart of Camus's philosophy lies the understanding that life is inherently absurd. He argues that the absurd arises from the clash between humanity's inherent desire for meaning and the indifferent universe that does not provide inherent meaning. In the face of this paradox, individuals are confronted with a choice: to live in despair or to embrace the absurd and create their own meaning. Camus's philosophy rejects the search for ultimate truth or rationality but instead focuses on the importance of authenticity and accepting life's inherent contradictions.

Existentialism, a philosophical movement prominent in the mid-20th century, aligns closely with Camus's ideas on the absurd. Existentialists, such as Jean-Paul Sartre and Simone dae Beauvoir, emphasise the individual's responsibility for creating meaning in a world devoid of objective purpose. They argue that human existence precedes essence, meaning that individuals first exist and then define their essence through their choices and actions.

However, Camus's philosophy distinguishes itself from traditional existentialism in some respects. While Sartre and de Beauvoir emphasise the freedom to choose one's path, Camus highlights the limits of human agency. In the face of an absurd and indifferent world, certain boundaries and limitations cannot be surpassed. This acknowledgement of the human condition led Camus to advocate for a philosophy of revolt, emphasising the importance of resisting unjust and meaningless situations while accepting the inherent limitations of existence.

Camus further explores his ideas in his famous essay, "The Myth of Sisyphus." In it, he introduces the mythological figure of Sisyphus, who the gods condemn to roll a boulder up a hill for eternity, only to watch it roll back down again. Camus sees Sisyphus as the absurd hero, tirelessly engaging in an act devoid of purpose. Despite the futility of his task, Sisyphus ultimately finds meaning and fulfilment in the absurdity of his existence. Camus argues that by embracing our own absurd condition, we can find a transcendent happiness that revolts against the meaninglessness of life.

Camus's exploration of the absurd and his rejection of traditional existentialist notions have profoundly impacted literature and philosophy. His philosophy resonates with individuals who experience life's inherent contradictions and absurdities, offering them a framework to navigate meaning and purpose in a world that often lacks both.

Moreover, Camus's impact extends beyond the realm of philosophy. His literature and ideas have influenced subsequent generations of writers, thinkers, and popular culture. Through his plays like Caligula and The Just Assassins, Camus explores the absurdity of power and the human potential for revolt. His works continue to challenge and provoke readers, inviting them to question the status quo and confront the absurdity of existence.

In conclusion, Albert Camus's exploration of the absurd and his contribution to existentialist thought has left an indelible mark on the intellectual landscape. Through his writings, he encourages individuals to embrace life's paradoxical nature, find meaning in the face of an indifferent universe, and revolt against injustice. His philosophy illuminates the complexity of human existence and inspires us to seek our own truths in a world that often presents us with absurd challenges. We can discover a profound sense of purpose and fulfilment by confronting the absurd and engaging in the revolt against meaninglessness.

Bibliography

For readers who wish to delve deeper into the works and ideas of Albert Camus, the following list of selected references provides a comprehensive and diverse selection for further exploration:

Albert 1913-1960 Camus, and Stuart Tr Gilbert. 2021. *Caligula and Cross Purpose (Le Malentendu)*. Hassell Street Press.

Alice Yaeger Kaplan. 2018. *Looking for the Stranger: Albert Camus and the Life of a Literary Classic*. Chicago University Of Chicago Press.

Aronson, Ronald. 2004. *Camus & Sartre: The Story of a Friendship and the Quarrel That Ended It*. Chicago: University Of Chicago Press.

Badiou Alain(2010), "The Rebel" London: Verso

Beauclair Michelle(1988) "Camus : fille de pauvre à écrivain mondial." Paris: Editions du Félin.

Bettina Liebowitz Knapp. 1988. *Critical Essays on Albert Camus*. Macmillan Reference USA.

Bloom, Harold. 2009. *The Stranger - Albert Camus*. Infobase Publishing.

Bloom, Harold. "Albert Camus." Broomall: Chelsea House Publishers, 2009.

Boisvert, Raymond D. 2023. *Albert Camus and the Philosophy of the Ordinary*. Bloomsbury Publishing.

Bowker, Matthew H. 2013a. *Albert Camus and the Political Philosophy of the Absurd: Ambivalence, Resistance, and Creativity*. Lanham: Lexington Books.

Bray, Patrick M (2012) "Understanding Albert Camus," University of South Carolina Press.

Brée Germain, (1964) "Albert Camus" : New York: Harcourt.

Brée Germaine(1971), "Camus", New York : Harcourt Brace Jovanovich.

Bronner, Stephen Eric. "Camus: Portrait of a Moralist." University of Chicago Press, 2009.

Camus Albert(1972), "Carnets", Paris:Gallimard.

Colonna Frédéric(2004)"Le Premier Homme d'Albert Camus",Présence africaine : Paris

Daoud, Kamel. "The Meursault Investigation." Pegasus Books, 2015.

Faucon Bernard (1989), "La mort heureuse : interprétation citée et commentée", Paris : Gallimard.

Froidefond Gaëtan,(2000), "Les Sources Grecques D'Albert Camus" Peter Lang France.

Gray David, (1972)"Albert Camus The Algerian" : Fort Worth: Texas Christian UP.

Kellman Steven G., (1980)"The Translingual Imagination": Lincoln University Nebraska Press.

Marcel Virginie (ed)(2005), "Albert Camus sa vie son oeuvre avec un exposé complet de toutes ses oeuvres", La Rochelle : Les éditions du temps.

McCarthy, Patrick. "Camus: A Critical Study of His Life and Work." Harvard University Press, 1982.

Mithra Madjid(1991)" La littérature selon Michel Arrivé,"Paris : PUF.

O'Brien Conor Cruise, (1970) "Albert Camus of Europe and Africa": New York, Viking.

Peterson, Dale (ed). "The Stranger: Humanity and the Absurd." Twayne Publishers,1997.

Qadéïmi Hassan Ed.(1978), "Etudes camusiennes", Casablanca : Publication de l'Université Sidi Mohamed Ben Abdallah.

Rhein, Philip. "Albert Camus." Stanford University Press, 2003.

Rigaud-Drayton Margaret(1996),"Albert Camus"Paris : Les Éditions du Seuil.

Sherman, David (ed). "Camus' challenge: The Phenomenology of the Body." Mariner Books,2000.

Sprinker, Michael (1992), "Modernism and Colonialism: Reading Joyce After Empire," Duke UP.

Srigley Ronald D (2010) "Camus' Critique of Modernity", University Of Missouri press.

Stirling Linda Ruth (1965), "Camus and Sartre": Crisis and Commitment', New York : DelacortePress

Todd Olivier(1979)"Albert Camus" ,Brussels: Éditions Complexe.

Todd Olivier (1998), "Albert Camus: Une Vie", Paris: Flammarion.

———. 2013b. *Rethinking the Politics of Absurdity*. Routledge.

Bright Summaries. 2016a. *The First Man by Albert Camus (Book Analysis)*. BrightSummaries.com.

Camus Society. 2013. *Journal of Camus Studies.* Lulu Com.

Camus, Albert. 1948. *Le Mythe de Sisyphe Par Albert Camus*. Gallimard.

———. 1960. *The Collected Fiction of Albert Camus.* London: Hamish Hamilton.

———. 1971. *La Mort Heureuse*. Editions Gallimard.

———. 1972. *L'étranger*. Gallimard.

———. (1947) 1991. *The Plague*. New York: Vintage Books, A Division Of Random House, Inc.

———. 2006. *The Fall*. Penguin Classics.

———. 2007. *Christian Metaphysics and Neoplatonism*. University of Missouri Press.

———. 2008. *La Peste*. Editions Gallimard.

———. 2010. *L'homme Révolté*. Paris: Gallimard.

———. 2012a. *Caligula and Three Other Plays*. Vintage.

———. 2012b. *The First Man*. Vintage.

———. 2012c. *Resistance, Rebellion, and Death*. Vintage.

———. 2012d. *The Myth of Sisyphus and Other Essays*. Vintage.

———. (1942) 2013. *The Stranger*. New York: Vintage International.

———. 2013a. *Algerian Chronicles*. Harvard University Press.

———. 2013b. *A Happy Death*. Penguin UK.

———. 2018. *(L'Etranger) the Outsider*. Bloomsbury Publishing.

———. 2022a. *Speaking Out*. Vintage.

———. 2022b. *Fiche de Lecture Le Mythe de Sisyphe de Albert Camus (Étude Intégrale)*. Paideia Education.

———. 2022c. *Le Mythe de Sisyphe*. DigiCat.

———. 2023. *Travels in the Americas*. University of Chicago Press.

Camus, Albert, and Christopher John Williams. 2007. *The Misunderstanding and Caligula*. Hobart, Tasmania: Knocklofty Press.

Camus, Albert, Sophie Doudet, and Alain Jaubert. 2008. *La Chute*. Editions Gallimard.

Camus, Albert, and Herbert Read. 2012. *The Rebel : An Essay on Man in Revolt*. New York: Vintage.

Camus, Albert, Philip Thody, and Kingsport Press. 1968. *Lyrical and Critical Essays.* New York, Knopf.

Camus, Catherine, Marcelle Mahasela, and Joseph Laredo. 2012. *Albert Camus : Solitude and Solidarity*. Zürich: Edition Olms.

Carroll, David. 2007. *Albert Camus the Algerian Colonialism, Terrorism, Justice*. Columbia University Press.

Catelli, Giovanni. 2021. *Death of Camus*. Oxford University Press.

Foley, John. 2008. *Albert Camus : From the Absurd to Revolt*. Stocksfield, Uk: Acumen.

Foxlee, Neil. 2010. *Albert Camus's "the New Mediterranean Culture" : A Text and Its Contexts*. Oxford ; New York: Peter Lang.

Francev, Peter. 2014a. *Albert Camus's the Stranger : Critical Essays*. Newcastle Upon Tyne, Uk: Cambridge Scholars.

———. 2014b. *Journal of Camus Studies 2014*. Camus Society.

Francev, Peter, and Maciej Kałuża. 2022. *Coming back to the Absurd: Albert Camus's the Myth of Sisyphus: 80 Years On*. BRILL.

Gale, Cengage Learning. 2015. *A Study Guide for Albert Camus's the Plague*. Gale, Cengage Learning.

Gloag, Oliver. 2019. *ALBERT CAMUS: A Very Short Introduction.* S.L.: Oxford Univ Press.

Hamid Nacer-Khodja. 2019. *Albert Camus, Jean Sénac, or the Rebel Son*. MSU Press.

Hawcroft, Michael. 1999. *Rhetoric: Readings in French Literature*. Oxford; New York: Oxford University Press.

Hawes, Elizabeth. 2010. *Camus, a Romance*. Open Road + Grove/Atlantic.

Hughes, Edward J. 2007. *The Cambridge Companion to Camus*. Cambridge University Press.

Jacqueline Gabrielle Roston. 1985. *Camus's Récit La Chute*. Peter Lang Gmbh, Internationaler Verlag Der Wissenschaften.

Jean-Bosco d'Otreppe, Johanna Biehler, and lePetitL itteraire.fr. 2017. *La Chute d'Albert Camus (Analyse de L'oeuvre)*. lePetitLitteraire.fr.

Jean-Marie Schaeffer, and Dorrit Claire Cohn. 2010. *Why Fiction? = Pourquoi La Fiction ?* Lincoln; London: University Of Nebraska Press. Copyright.

Jean-Paul Sartre. (1943) 1999. *Being and Nothingness: A Phenomenological Essay on Ontology.* New York, NY: Washington Square Press.

Jean-Paul Sartre, Ronald Aronson, and Adrian Van. 2013. *We Have Only This Life to Live: Selected Essays of Jean-Paul Sartre, 1939-1975*. New York, NY: New York Review Books.

Jean-Paul Sartre, and Albert Camus. 2004. *Sartre and Camus*. Humanities Press International.

Jones, Rosemarie. 1994. *Camus, L'étranger and La Chute*. Foyles.

King, Adele. 1992. *Camus's L'Etranger: Fifty Years On*. Springer.

Lempert, Manya. 2020. *Tragedy and the Modernist Novel*. Cambridge; New York: Cambridge University Press.

Lottman, Herbert R. 1997. *Albert Camus : A Biography*. Corte Madera, California: Gingko Press.

Margerrison, Christine. 2008. *"Ces Forces Obscures de L'âme" : Women, Race and Origins in the Writings of Albert Camus*. Amsterdam; New York: Rodopi.

McBride, J. 2016. *Albert Camus*. Springer.

Nelson, Brian. 2015. *The Cambridge Introduction to French Literature*. CUP.

Orme, Mark. 2007. *The Development of Albert Camus's Concern for Social and Political Justice: "Justice Pour Un Juste."* Madison: Fairleigh Dickinson University Press.

Peg Brand Weiser. 2023. *Camus's the Plague*. Oxford University Press.

Pierre-Georges Castex. 1986. *Albert Camus et "L'Étranger."* Paris: J. Corti.

Sagi, Avi. 2022. *Albert Camus and the Philosophy of the Absurd*. BRILL.

Schellinger, Paul. 2014. *Encyclopedia of the Novel*. Routledge.

Sharpe, Matthew, KałużaMaciej, and Peter Francev. 2020. *Brill's Companion to Camus: Camus among the Philosophers*. Leiden: Brill.

Sherman, David. 2009. *Camus*. John Wiley & Sons.

Summaries, Bright. 2016b. *The Myth of Sisyphus by Albert Camus (Book Analysis) Detailed Summary, Analysis and Reading Guide*. Namur: Lemaitre Publishing.

Sung-Eun Choi. 2016. *Decolonization and the French of Algeria Bringing the Settler Colony Home*. London Palgrave Macmillan UK:Imprint: Palgrave Macmillan.

Team, IntroBooks. n.d. *Albert Camus' Philosophy*. IntroBooks.

Trundle, Robert C, and R Puligandla. 1987. *Beyond Absurdity: The Philosophy of Albert Camus*. London: University Press Of America.

Van, Adrian, and Andrew N Leak. 2005. *Sartre Today: A Centenary Celebration*. New York: Berghahn Books.

Wallace, Dave. 2017. *The Rebel Summary & Analysis*. Createspace Independent Publishing Platform.

Whistler, Grace. 2020. *Camus' Literary Ethics*. Springer Nature.

Woelfel, James W. 1987. *Albert Camus on the Sacred and the Secular*. University Press of Amer.

Zaretsky, Robert. 2013. *A Life Worth Living*. Harvard University Press.

www.ingramcontent.com/pod-product-compliance
Lightning Source LLC
Chambersburg PA
CBHW070352200726
48294CB00003B/864

* 9 7 8 1 7 8 7 9 5 0 7 7 1 *